Ninja Foodi

Cold & Hot Blender cookbook for Beginners 2024

Yummy and Fresh Recipes for Smoothies, Soups, Sauces, Infused Cocktails, and More

DANIELLA B. JONES

TABLE OF CONTENTS

Chapter 6: Baby Food Purees

Chapter 7: Blender Baking

Chapter 8: Savory Blender Mains 59

Chapter 9: Superfood Boosters 66

Chapter 10: Sips & Tonics 71

Nutritional Informations 76

INTRODUCTION TO THE NINJA FOODI COLD & HOT BLENDER

What is it and how does it work?

As a passionate home cook and kitchen gadget enthusiast, I've tried my fair share of blenders over the years. But when the Ninja Foodi Cold & Hot Blender landed on my countertop, it was a total game-changer. This versatile powerhouse is so much more than just a blender – it's a complete culinary workstation that simplifies meal prep and opens up a world of possibilities in the kitchen.

At its core, the Ninja Foodi Cold & Hot Blender is a high-performance blender that can pulverise even the toughest ingredients into velvety smooth textures. But what sets it apart is its ability to not only blend cold ingredients but also heat them to a piping-hot temperature, all in the same container. This dual functionality is made possible by the blender's built-in heating element and precise temperature control.

The blending process is incredibly simple: just add your ingredients to the blender jug, select your desired setting (cold blend, hot blend, or a pre-programmed function), and let the powerful motor and specialised blades do their magic. Within minutes, you'll have a perfectly blended concoction, whether it's a frosty smoothie, a steaming hot soup, or anything in between.

But the Ninja Foodi Cold & Hot Blender isn't just about blending – it's a true culinary multi-tasker. With its versatile functions and customisable settings, you can use it to make everything from nut butter and homemade baby food to dips, sauces, and even batter for baked goods. The possibilities are virtually endless!

Features and Benefits

The Ninja Foodi Cold & Hot Blender is packed with features that make it a standout addition to any kitchen. Here are just a few of the key benefits that have made it a favourite among home cooks and professional chefs alike:

Dual Functionality: As mentioned, the ability to blend both cold and hot ingredients in the same jug is a game-changer. No more transferring hot liquids from a pot to a separate blender – the Ninja does it all in one vessel.

Powerful Motor: With a robust 1,400-watt motor, this blender can tackle even the toughest ingredients with ease. Say goodbye to chunky, uneven textures and hello to silky smooth results every time.

Precision Temperature Control: When blending hot ingredients, you can easily adjust the temperature in 5-degree increments, allowing you to achieve the perfect consistency for soups, sauces, and more.

Pre-Programmed Settings: Take the guesswork out of blending with pre-programmed settings for smoothies, spreads, hot soups, and more. Just press a button, and the blender will automatically adjust the blend time and speed for optimal results.

Blending Cup Accessories: In addition to the main blender jug, the Ninja Foodi Cold & Hot Blender comes with two single-serve cups, perfect for whipping up personal smoothies or protein shakes on the go.

Easy Cleaning: The blender jug, blades, and accessories are all dishwasher-safe, making cleanup a breeze. Plus, the sleek design and smooth surfaces prevent messy spills and splatters.

Versatility: From hot soups and sauces to frozen desserts and cocktails, this blender can handle it all. Its versatility means you'll be using it for a wide range of recipes, making it a true workhorse in your kitchen.

Different Models and Accessories

The Ninja Foodi Cold & Hot Blender is available in several different models, each designed to cater to various household sizes and cooking needs. Here's a quick overview of the different options:

Ninja Foodi Cold & Hot Blender (Model HB152): This is the standard model and includes the following:

1.6L blender jug with tamper

Two 600ml single-serve cups with to-go lids

Recipe book

Ninja Foodi Cold & Hot Blender Deluxe (Model HB153): In addition to the standard components, this deluxe model also includes:

1.4L precision processor bowl for chopping, dicing, and pureeing

Dough blade for kneading bread dough

Ninja Foodi Cold & Hot Blender with Auto-IQ (Model HB154): This top-of-the-line model features advanced Auto-IQ technology that automatically adjusts the blending pattern, speed, and timing for optimal results. It includes:

1.6L blender jug with tamper

Two 600ml single-serve cups with to-go lids

Parts of the Blender and Their Functions

Let's start by taking a closer look at the various components that make up the Ninja Foodi Cold & Hot Blender:

Motor Base: This is the heart of the blender, housing the powerful motor that drives the blades. It's where you'll find the control panel and various settings.

Blender Jug: The blender jug is the main vessel where all the blending magic happens. It's made of durable, shatter-proof plastic and features a comfortable handle and pour spout for easy serving.

Tamper: The tamper is a long, cylindrical tool that you can use to push ingredients towards the blades while the blender is running. This helps ensure even blending and prevents air pockets from forming.

Blades: The Ninja Foodi Cold & Hot Blender is equipped with specialised blades that are designed to pulverise ingredients with precision. The blades are made of high-quality stainless steel and are incredibly sharp, so handle them with care.

Single-Serve Cups: In addition to the main blender jug, the Ninja Foodi comes with two single-serve cups, perfect for blending up individual smoothies or shakes on the go.

Control Panel and Settings: The control panel is where you'll find all the buttons and settings for operating the blender. We'll dive into these in more detail in the next section.

Control Panel and Settings

The control panel on the Ninja Foodi Cold & Hot Blender may seem a bit intimidating at first, with its array of buttons and settings. But don't worry – it's quite user-friendly once you understand what each feature does. Here's a breakdown of the main settings:

Cold Blend: This setting is for blending cold ingredients, such as smoothies, milkshakes, and frozen desserts. It provides a powerful, high-speed blend for achieving smooth, frosty textures.

Hot Blend: As the name suggests, this setting is for blending hot ingredients, like soups, sauces, and purees. It combines the blending power with a heating element to bring the contents to a piping-hot temperature.

Temperature Control: When using the Hot Blend setting, you can precisely adjust the temperature in 5-degree increments, ranging from 105°F to 205°F (40°C to 96°C). This level of control allows you to achieve the perfect consistency for your desired recipe.

Pre-Programmed Settings: The Ninja Foodi Cold & Hot Blender also features a range of pre-programmed settings that take the guesswork out of blending. These include options for smoothies, spreads, hot soups, and more. Simply press the corresponding button, and the blender will automatically adjust the blending time, speed, and temperature for optimal results

Safety Precautions

Before we dive into using the Ninja Foodi, it's important to go over some essential safety guidelines. While this blender is incredibly user-friendly, it's still a powerful appliance that requires proper handling and care. Here are some key safety tips to keep in mind:

Read the manual: I know, I know – no one really likes reading instruction manuals. But trust me, it's worth taking the time to familiarize yourself with the specific safety guidelines and operating instructions for your Ninja Foodi model.

Handle with care: Those blender blades are seriously sharp, so always exercise caution when handling them. Never try to remove the blades from the jug or place your hands too close to the blades when the blender is plugged in.

Hot liquids: When blending hot liquids or ingredients, always use the vented lid cap to allow steam to escape. Hot liquids can build up pressure, so start on a low setting and gradually increase the speed.

Keep it steady: During operation, make sure the blender base is on a flat, stable surface to prevent it from tipping or moving around.

Unplug when not in use: This may seem obvious, but it's an important safety measure. Always unplug the blender from the power source when you're not using it, and before cleaning or disassembling any parts.

Avoid immersion: Never submerge the motor base in water or any other liquid, as this could cause electrical damage or shock.

Why Blend?

Now that we've covered the basics, let's talk about why blending is such an amazing technique to incorporate into your cooking routine. Sure, a high-performance blender like the Ninja Foodi is a fantastic appliance to have, but what are the real benefits of blending? Here are just a few reasons why I'm such a big advocate for embracing the blending lifestyle:

Nutritional Powerhouse: Blending is an incredibly efficient way to pack in a ton of nutrients from fresh fruits, vegetables, and other wholesome ingredients. By breaking down the cell walls of these nutritious foods, blending helps to unlock and make their vitamins, minerals, and antioxidants more bioavailable for our bodies to absorb.

Increased Fiber: Most of us could use a little extra fibre in our diets, and blending is a great way to get it. When you blend up fruits and veggies with their skins and seeds intact, you're retaining all that valuable fiber that can aid in digestion and promote overall gut health.

Easy Meal Prep: Let's face it – life can get busy, and finding the time to prepare healthy meals from scratch isn't always easy. With a blender like the Ninja Foodi, you can quickly whip up nutrient-dense smoothies, soups, and sauces that make meal prep a breeze.

Reduced Food Waste: Have you ever let fresh produce go bad because you didn't have a chance to use it up? By blending up those slightly overripe fruits and wilted veggies, you can transform them into delicious drinks, dips, or purees, reducing food waste and saving money in the process.

Versatility: From silky smooth soups and creamy dips to decadent desserts and refreshing cocktails, a high-performance blender like the Ninja Foodi can tackle an incredible range of recipes. With just one versatile appliance, you can expand your culinary horizons and explore new flavours and textures.

But perhaps the biggest reason to embrace blending is the sheer joy and satisfaction it can bring to your cooking experience. There's something incredibly satisfying about creating a vibrant, nutrient-packed blend from scratch and knowing that you're nourishing your body with wholesome, delicious ingredients. Trust me; once you start blending, you'll be hooked!

Choosing the Right Ingredients

One of the keys to successful blending is selecting the right ingredients. While the Ninja Foodi Cold & Hot Blender can pulverize just about anything you throw into it, certain ingredients will yield better textures, flavours, and overall results than others. Here are some tips on choosing the best ingredients for your blending adventures:

Fresh vs. Frozen Produce: When it comes to fruits and veggies, both fresh and frozen options can work well in the blender. Fresh produce will generally have a brighter, more vibrant flavour, while frozen can be more convenient and cost-effective, especially when certain items are out of season. If using frozen, look for options without any added syrups or sugars.

Leafy Greens: Blending is an excellent way to sneak more greens into your diet. Spinach, kale, and other leafy greens blend beautifully into smoothies, juices, and soups. For the best texture, start with just a handful and gradually add more as you get used to the taste and consistency.

Fruits: Fruits are a blender's best friend, adding natural sweetness, fibre, and a host of vitamins and antioxidants to your blends. Some great options include bananas (which also add creaminess), berries, mangoes, pineapples, and citrus fruits like oranges and grapefruits.

Healthy Fats: To create thick, creamy textures and add a satisfying richness to your blends, incorporate healthy fats like avocados, nuts, nut butter, seeds, and coconut products.

Protein Sources: Blending is a convenient way to boost your protein intake, whether you're looking for a post-workout recovery shake or a filling, nutrient-dense meal replacement. Try adding protein powders, Greek yoghurt, silken tofu, or even cooked meats or legumes.

Boosters and Extras: Have some fun playing around with different flavour boosters and mix-ins like spices, extracts, fresh herbs, nut butter, and even coffee or tea for an extra kick of flavour and nutrition.

Remember, the beauty of blending is that you can customize your creations to suit your tastes and dietary needs. Don't be afraid to experiment and find your favourite flavour combinations!

Prepping Like a Pro

Now that you understand the importance of choosing the right ingredients, let's talk about how to properly prepare for your blending sessions. A little bit of prep work can go a long way in ensuring smooth, efficient blending and delicious results every time.

Proper Cleaning and Maintenance

Before we get o into prepping ingredients, let's quickly cover some basics on keeping your Ninja Foodi Clean & Hot Blender in tip-top shape. Proper cleaning and maintenance are key to ensuring your blender performs at its best and has a long, useful life.

The blender jug, tamper, single-serve cups, and lids are all dishwasher-safe for easy cleaning. However, I recommend giving them a quick rinse or soak immediately after use to prevent any stuck-on messes from drying and becoming more difficult to remove.

For the motor base, simply wipe it down with a damp cloth to keep it clean. Never submerge the motor base in water or put it in the dishwasher, as this could damage the electrical components. It's also a good idea to periodically clean the blades and remove any built-up residue. To do this, fill the blender halfway with warm water and a drop of dish soap, then blend on a low speed for 30 seconds to 1 minute. This will help dislodge any stubborn bits. Rinse thoroughly with clean water. Finally, be sure to check your blender blades regularly for any signs of dullness or damage. While the Ninja Foodi's blades are incredibly durable, they may eventually need to be replaced after years of heavy use.

Mise en Place for Efficient Blending

Any good chef will tell you that proper preparation, or "mise en place," is key to efficient cooking and successful results. The same principle applies to blending.

Before you start blending, take a few minutes to gather and prepare all of your ingredients. This could involve washing and drying your produce, measuring out ingredients, chopping larger items into smaller pieces, or even portioning out ingredients if you're making multiple batches.

Having everything ready to go prevents you from having to stop mid-blend to prep something, which can disrupt the blending process and lead to uneven textures. It also just makes the whole experience more enjoyable and stress-free when you're not scrambling to find or prepare ingredients.

Here are some additional mise en place tips for efficient blending:

Layer ingredients properly in the blender jug based on density (more on this in the next section)

If making smoothies or shakes, add any powders (protein, greens, etc.) first so they get fully incorporated

For hot blends, have all ingredients at room temperature to prevent shocking the blades with extreme temperatures

Keep a cup of liquid (milk, juice, broth, etc.) on hand to add if blends become too thick

With your ingredients prepped and ready to go, you'll be able to blend like a pro and achieve those beautifully smooth, lump-free results every time.

Storage Tips for Blended Items

Part of what makes blending so convenient is that you can easily prepare batches of items like smoothies, sauces, dips, or purees in advance for quick meals and snacks throughout the week. However, it's important to store your blended creations properly to maintain freshness, flavor, and nutrients. Here are some handy storage tips:

Smoothies & Shakes: Pour your smoothies into air-tight jars or bottles with minimal air space at the top. They'll keep fresh in the fridge for 1-2 days. For longer storage of up to a week, freeze in portions using zip-top bags or silicone freezer trays.

Soups & Sauces: Allow hot soups and sauces to cool completely before transferring to air-tight containers or jars. They'll keep in the fridge for 3-4 days. For longer storage of up to 3 months, cool thoroughly and freeze in portions.

Dips & Spreads: Most dips and nut/seed butter spreads will be kept in the fridge for up to a week in an air-tight container. For longer storage, portion into smaller containers with a tight seal and freeze for 2-3 months.

Baby Purees: Baby food purees can be refrigerated for 3 days, or frozen for up to 3 months. Freeze in ice cube trays or small containers, leaving a bit of room for expansion.

No matter what you're blending up, be sure to let hot items cool completely before refrigerating or freezing to prevent bacteria growth. Defrost frozen items overnight in the fridge rather than at room temperature.

Proper storage is key to making your blends last and maintaining those fresh flavours and vibrant colours. With these tips, you'll always have healthy, homemade treats on hand!

Layering Ingredients Properly

One final tip for successful blending: layering your ingredients properly in the blender jug or cup. This may seem like a minor detail, but it can actually make a big difference in your final textures and how easily the blender can do its job.

The basic principle is to load ingredients into the blender from most dense to least dense. This allows the denser items to get pulled towards the blades first while preventing lighter, airier ingredients from getting trapped underneath.

Here's how I recommend layering ingredients for different types of blends:

For Smoothies/Shakes:

Powders or boosters (protein, greens, etc.)
Dense ingredients (frozen fruits, nuts, nut butter)
Fresh fruits and vegetables
Leafy greens
Liquids (milk, juice, yoghurt)
Ice or frozen ingredients
For Hot Soups/Sauces:
Denser veggies (potatoes, squash, etc.)
Lighter veggies and herbs
Liquids (broth, milk, etc.)

For Dips/Nut Butters:

Nuts/seeds
Additions like garlic, spices, etc.
Liquids (oil, milk, etc.) as needed

Within each category, arrange from biggest to smallest pieces so that larger items get blended first. And be sure not to overfill the blender jug or cup - leave a bit of room at the top for ingredients to move around.

By taking just a minute to strategically layer your ingredients, you'll find that your blender can work more efficiently, resulting in smoother, more evenly blended textures every time.

Blending Techniques

Now that you've got all the basics down, it's time to dive into some specific techniques to help you master cold and hot blending with your Ninja Foodi. While this powerful blender makes the process pretty straightforward, there are still some tips and tricks that can take your blends to the next level.

Achieving Perfect Textures

One of the biggest challenges when blending can be achieving that perfect, velvety smooth texture you're going for, whether it's a creamy smoothie or a velvety soup. Here are some of my go-to techniques for banishing lumps and grittiness:

Use the Tamper: That cylindrical tamper tool may seem basic, but it's your secret weapon for smooth blending. As the blender is running, you can use the tamper to push ingredients into the blades and prevent air pockets from forming. This ensures everything gets thoroughly incorporated.

Go in Stages: For very thick or dense blends, I like to start on a lower speed to grind down the ingredients a bit first. Then, I'll gradually increase to higher speeds to fully puree everything into that perfect, smooth texture.

Blend Longer: Don't be afraid to let your Ninja Foodi run for a little longer than you think is needed, especially for things like nut butter or green smoothies. That extra blending time helps to break everything down into an ultra-smooth consistency.

Add Liquid: If a blend seems too thick or gets stuck, adding a splash of liquid like milk, juice, or broth can help loosen it up and get everything moving again for smoother blending.

Strain if Needed: For ultra-silky results, you can always pour your blend through a mesh strainer to remove any remaining gritty bits or pulp if desired. This works well for velvety smooth soups or juices.

With a little patience and these texture-perfecting tips, you'll be a smoothie-sipping, soup-slurping pro in no time!

Hot Blending vs. Cold Blending

One of the unique features of the Ninja Foodi is its ability to blend both cold and hot ingredients with precision. While the general blending motion is the same, there are some specific techniques to get the best results for hot and cold blends.

For Cold Blends:

Start with all ingredients chilled or at room temp (adding very hot items to a cold blend can cause splattering)

If using frozen fruits or ingredients, you may need to add more liquid to get things moving

Use the tamper frequently to incorporate frozen chunks into the blend

For thicker blends like nut butter, you may need to stop and scrape down the sides periodically

For frozen desserts, solidify churned mixtures in the freezer after blending for the best texture

For Hot Blends:

Always vent the lid by removing the cap to allow steam to escape

Start on one of the lower speed settings when blending gets hot to prevent splattering

Use the tamper cautiously when blending hot liquids to avoid burns

For chunky soups and sauces, do an initial cold blend first, then switch to hot blend mode

Fill the jug no more than halfway when blending hot items to allow room for expansion

Use caution when removing the lid or handling the jug after hot blending - the contents will be very hot!

No matter if you're blending hot or cold, I always recommend starting the Ninja on a lower speed and then working your way up to higher speeds. This helps incorporate ingredients more evenly. Understanding the subtle differences between these two blending modes will help you get perfect, consistent results every time.

Layering Ingredients Properly

You'll recall that in the prepping section, we discussed the importance of layering ingredients properly in the blender jug based on their density. This is worth revisiting as an essential blending technique.

As a general rule of thumb, you'll want to start with your densest, heaviest ingredients at the bottom of the jug. This allows the blades to easily catch and grind through those items first. From there, layer upwards from dense to light ingredients, finishing with any liquids or frozen items on top.

Here's an example of how I would layer ingredients for a classic green smoothie:

Protein powder, seeds, nuts

Dense fruits like bananas, pineapple chunks

Leafy greens like kale or spinach

Fresh berries or chopped fruits

Liquids like milk, juice, yoghurt

Any ice or frozen ingredients

Ordering your layers this way not only makes it easier on the blades, but it also prevents issues like liquid sloshing out the top or frozen chunks getting stuck underneath.

For hot blends like soups and sauces, I start with very dense veggies on the bottom, then layer upwards with lighter veggies, herbs, and finally any cooking liquids on top.

The tamper can also be a huge help when it comes to keeping things moving in those proper layers as you're blending up a storm.

Trust me, once you get in the habit of strategic layering, you'll notice a world of difference in your blending results. Those pesky stuck blends and air pockets will be a thing of the past!

With these pro blending techniques under your belt, you are officially a Ninja Foodi Blending Master! From achieving that perfect velvety texture to understanding the differences between hot and cold blending modes, you've got all the skills to start cranking out some seriously impressive blends.

In the next chapter, we'll cover how to incorporate the Ninja Foodi into your day-to-day meal planning for quick, healthy meals and snacks. We'll also provide some guidance on calculating nutritional information and catering to dietary restrictions.

Tropical Green Smoothie

Prep: 5 mins | Serves: 2

Ingredients:

US: 2 cups spinach leaves, 1 cup pineapple chunks (frozen), 1 banana, ½ cup coconut milk, ½ cup orange juice, 1 tablespoon honey

UK: 200g spinach leaves, 200g pineapple chunks (frozen), 1 banana, 120ml coconut milk, 120ml orange juice, 15g honey

Instructions:

1. Add spinach, pineapple chunks, banana, coconut milk, orange juice, and honey to the Ninja Foodi Cold & Hot Blender.
2. Select the "Smoothie" function and blend until smooth.
3. Pour into glasses and serve immediately for a refreshing tropical boost.

Nutritional Info: Calories: 160 | Fat: 3g | Carbs: 35g | Protein: 3g

Chocolate Peanut Butter Protein Shake

Prep: 5 mins | Serves: 2

Ingredients:

US: 2 tablespoons cocoa powder, 2 tablespoons peanut butter, 1 scoop chocolate protein powder, 1 banana, 1 cup almond milk, 1 cup ice cubes

UK: 25g cocoa powder, 30g peanut butter, 1 scoop chocolate protein powder, 1 banana, 240ml almond milk, 150g ice cubes

Instructions:

1. Combine cocoa powder, peanut butter, chocolate protein powder, banana, almond milk, and ice cubes in the Ninja Foodi Cold & Hot Blender.
2. Choose the "Smoothie" function and blend until creamy.
3. Pour into glasses and enjoy this protein-packed indulgence.

Nutritional Info: Calories: 280 | Fat: 11g | Carbs: 26g | Protein: 22g

Triple Berry Blitz

Prep: 5 mins | Serves: 2
Ingredients:
US: 1 cup mixed berries (strawberries, blueberries, raspberries), ½ cup Greek yogurt, ½ cup coconut water, 1 tablespoon honey, 1 cup ice cubes
UK: 150g mixed berries (strawberries, blueberries, raspberries), 120g Greek yogurt, 120ml coconut water, 15g honey, 150g ice cubes
Instructions:
1. Place mixed berries, Greek yogurt, coconut water, honey, and ice cubes into the Ninja Foodi Cold & Hot Blender.
2. Select the "Smoothie" function and blend until smooth.
3. Pour into glasses and savor the burst of berry goodness.

Nutritional Info: Calories: 120 | Fat: 1g | Carbs: 26g | Protein: 4g

Zingy Beet Smoothie

Prep: 5 mins | Serves: 2
Ingredients:
US: 1 small cooked beetroot, 1 apple (cored and chopped), 1 carrot (peeled and chopped), ½ cup orange juice, ½ cup plain yoghurt, 1 tablespoon honey

UK: 100g cooked beetroot, 1 apple (cored and chopped), 1 carrot (peeled and chopped), 120ml orange juice, 120ml plain yoghurt, 15g honey

Instructions:
1. Add cooked beetroot, chopped apple, carrot, orange juice, yoghurt, and honey to the Ninja Foodi Cold & Hot Blender.
2. Choose the "Smoothie" function and blend until velvety.
3. Pour into glasses and relish the vibrant, zesty flavours.

Nutritional Info: Calories: 160 | Fat: 1g | Carbs: 36g | Protein: 4g

Peanut Butter & Banana Thickshake

Prep: 5 mins | Serves: 2
Ingredients:

US: 2 bananas, 2 tablespoons peanut butter, 1 cup milk, 1 teaspoon vanilla extract, 1 tablespoon honey, 1 cup ice cubes

UK: 2 bananas, 30g peanut butter, 240ml milk, 5ml vanilla extract, 15g honey, 150g ice cubes

Instructions:

1. Place bananas, peanut butter, milk, vanilla extract, honey, and ice cubes into the Ninja Foodi Cold & Hot Blender.
2. Select the "Smoothie" function and blend until thick and creamy.
3. Pour into glasses and enjoy the classic combination of peanut butter and banana.

Nutritional Info: Calories: 280 | Fat: 9g | Carbs: 45g | Protein: 9g

Mango Lassi

Prep: 5 mins | Serves: 2
Ingredients:

US: 1 cup diced mango, 1 cup plain yoghurt, ½ cup milk, 2 tablespoons honey, ½ teaspoon ground cardamom, 1 cup ice cubes

UK: 200g diced mango, 240ml plain yoghurt, 120ml milk, 30g honey, 2.5ml ground cardamom, 150g ice cubes

Instructions:

1. Add diced mango, yoghurt, milk, honey, ground cardamom, and ice cubes to the Ninja Foodi Cold & Hot Blender.
2. Choose the "Smoothie" function and blend until creamy and frothy.
3. Pour into glasses and transport yourself to the tropics with this refreshing mango delight.

Nutritional Info: Calories: 180 | Fat: 2g | Carbs: 39g | Protein: 6g

Mocha Avocado Shake

Prep: 5 mins | Serves: 2
Ingredients:

US: 1 ripe avocado, 2 tablespoons cocoa powder, 2 tablespoons instant coffee powder, 2 tablespoons honey, 1 cup milk, 1 cup ice cubes

UK: 1 ripe avocado, 25g cocoa powder, 25g instant coffee powder, 30g honey, 240ml milk, 150g ice cubes

Instructions:

1. Combine ripe avocado, cocoa powder, instant coffee powder, honey, milk, and ice cubes in the Ninja Foodi Cold & Hot Blender.
2. Select the "Smoothie" function and blend until smooth and creamy.
3. Pour into glasses and enjoy the rich, indulgent flavours of mocha and avocado.

Nutritional Info: Calories: 280 | Fat: 12g | Carbs: 38g | Protein: 6g

Green Detox Tonic

Prep: 5 mins | Serves: 2
Ingredients:

US: 2 cups kale leaves, 1 cucumber (peeled and chopped), 1 green apple (cored and chopped), ½ lemon (juiced), ½-inch piece of ginger (peeled), 1 cup coconut water, 1 cup ice cubes

UK: 100g kale leaves, 1 cucumber (peeled and chopped), 1 green apple (cored and chopped), ½ lemon (juiced), 1.25cm piece of ginger (peeled), 240ml coconut water, 150g ice cubes

Instructions:

1. Add kale leaves, chopped cucumber, apple, lemon juice, ginger, coconut water, and ice cubes to the Ninja Foodi Cold & Hot Blender.
2. Choose the "Smoothie" function and blend until vibrant green and smooth.
3. Pour into glasses and revitalize your body with this detoxifying green tonic.

Nutritional Info: Calories: 100 | Fat: 1g | Carbs: 24g | Protein: 3g

Dragonfruit Smoothie Bowl

Prep: 5 mins | Serves: 2
Ingredients:

US: 1 dragonfruit (peeled and chopped), 1 frozen banana, ½ cup coconut milk, ½ cup Greek yoghurt, 1 tablespoon honey, toppings of choice (granola, sliced fruit, coconut flakes)

UK: 1 dragonfruit (peeled and chopped), 1 frozen banana, 120ml coconut milk, 120ml Greek yoghurt, 15g honey, toppings of choice (granola, sliced fruit, coconut flakes)

Instructions:

1. Place chopped dragonfruit, frozen banana, coconut milk, Greek yogurt, and honey into the Ninja Foodi Cold & Hot Blender.
2. Select the "Smoothie" function and blend until thick and smooth.
3. Pour into bowls and top with granola, sliced fruit, and coconut flakes for a vibrant and nutritious breakfast or snack.

Nutritional Info: Calories: 220 | Fat: 4g | Carbs: 43g | Protein: 7g

Coffee Banana Cashew Shake

Prep: 5 mins | Serves: 2
Ingredients:

US: 2 bananas, 2 tablespoons cashew butter, 1 cup brewed coffee (chilled), ½ cup milk, 1 tablespoon maple syrup, 1 cup ice cubes

UK: 2 bananas, 30g cashew butter, 240ml brewed coffee (chilled), 120ml milk, 15g maple syrup, 150g ice cubes

Instructions:

1. Combine bananas, cashew butter, chilled brewed coffee, milk, maple syrup, and ice cubes in the Ninja Foodi Cold & Hot Blender.
2. Choose the "Smoothie" function and blend until creamy and frothy.
3. Pour into glasses and enjoy the energizing combination of coffee, banana, and cashew.

Nutritional Info: Calories: 240 | Fat: 6g | Carbs: 46g | Protein: 4g

Chapter 2: Juices & Nut Milks

Beginner's Delight

Prep: 5 mins | Serves: 2
Ingredients:

US: 2 oranges (peeled and segmented), 1 apple (cored and chopped), 1 carrot (peeled and chopped), ½ lemon (peeled and seeded), 1-inch piece of ginger (peeled), 1 cup cold water, 1 cup ice cubes

UK: 2 oranges (peeled and segmented), 1 apple (cored and chopped), 1 carrot (peeled and chopped), ½ lemon (peeled and seeded), 2.5cm piece of ginger (peeled), 240ml cold water, 150g ice cubes

Instructions:

1. Place oranges, apples, carrots, lemon, ginger, cold water, and ice cubes into the Ninja Foodi Cold & Hot Blender.
2. Select the "Juice" function and blend until smooth.
3. Pour into glasses and enjoy this refreshing and vibrant juice.

Nutritional Info: Calories: 90 | Fat: 0g | Carbs: 22g | Protein: 2g

Sunrise Zinger

Prep: 5 mins | Serves: 2
Ingredients:

US: 2 oranges (peeled and segmented), 1 grapefruit (peeled and segmented), 1 lemon (peeled and seeded), 1-inch piece of turmeric (peeled), 1 cup cold water, 1 cup ice cubes

UK: 2 oranges (peeled and segmented), 1 grapefruit (peeled and segmented), 1 lemon (peeled and seeded), 2.5cm piece of turmeric (peeled), 240ml cold water, 150g ice cubes

Instructions:

1. Add oranges, grapefruit, lemon, turmeric, cold water, and ice cubes to the Ninja Foodi Cold & Hot Blender.
2. Choose the "Juice" function and blend until well combined.
3. Pour into glasses and kick-start your day with this zesty, immune-boosting elixir.

Nutritional Info: Calories: 70 | Fat: 0g | Carbs: 17g | Protein: 2g

Tropi-Kale Juice

Prep: 5 mins | Serves: 2
Ingredients:

US: 2 cups kale leaves, 1 cup pineapple chunks (frozen), 1 banana, ½ cup coconut water, ½ cup orange juice, 1 tablespoon honey, 1 cup ice cubes

UK: 100g kale leaves, 200g pineapple chunks (frozen), 1 banana, 120ml coconut water, 120ml orange juice, 15g honey, 150g ice cubes

Instructions:

1. Place kale leaves, pineapple chunks, banana, coconut water, orange juice, honey, and ice cubes into the Ninja Foodi Cold & Hot Blender.
2. Select the "Juice" function and blend until smooth.
3. Pour into glasses and enjoy the tropical goodness of this nutritious green juice.

Nutritional Info: Calories: 150 | Fat: 1g | Carbs: 36g | Protein: 3g

Creamy Almond Milk

Prep: 10 mins | Serves: 4
Ingredients:

US: 1 cup almonds (soaked overnight), 4 cups water, 1 teaspoon vanilla extract, 1 tablespoon maple syrup

UK: 150g almonds (soaked overnight), 960ml water, 5ml vanilla extract, 15g maple syrup

Instructions:

1. Drain soaked almonds and rinse under cold water.
2. Place almonds, water, vanilla extract, and maple syrup into the Ninja Foodi Cold & Hot Blender.
3. Choose the "Nut Milk" function and blend until smooth.
4. Strain the mixture through a nut milk bag or fine sieve into a clean container.
5. Store in the refrigerator for up to 5 days and shake well before using.

Nutritional Info: Calories: 40 | Fat: 3g | Carbs: 2g | Protein: 1g

Rich Cashew Milk

Prep: 10 mins (+soaking) | Serves: 4
Ingredients:

US: 1 cup cashews (soaked overnight), 4 cups water, 1 teaspoon vanilla extract, 1 tablespoon honey

UK: 150g cashews (soaked overnight), 960ml water, 5ml vanilla extract, 15g honey

Instructions:

1. Drain soaked cashews and rinse under cold water.
2. Combine cashews, water, vanilla extract, and honey in the Ninja Foodi Cold & Hot Blender.
3. Select the "Nut Milk" function and blend until creamy.
4. Strain the mixture through a nut milk bag or fine sieve into a clean container.
5. Refrigerate and use within 3-4 days, shaking well before each use.

Nutritional Info: Calories: 50 | Fat: 3g | Carbs: 4g | Protein: 2g

Watermelon Mint Refresher

Prep: 5 mins | Serves: 2
Ingredients:

US: 2 cups cubed watermelon, 1 tablespoon fresh mint leaves, ½ lime (juiced), 1 cup cold water, 1 cup ice cubes

UK: 300g cubed watermelon, 15g fresh mint leaves, ½ lime (juiced), 240ml cold water, 150g ice cubes

Instructions:

1. Add cubed watermelon, mint leaves, lime juice, cold water, and ice cubes to the Ninja Foodi Cold & Hot Blender.
2. Choose the "Juice" function and blend until smooth.
3. Pour into glasses and enjoy the hydrating and refreshing taste of summer.

Nutritional Info: Calories: 45 | Fat: 0g | Carbs: 12g | Protein: 1g

Ruby Root Juice

Prep: 5 mins | Serves: 2
Ingredients:

US: 2 medium beetroots (peeled and chopped), 2 carrots (peeled and chopped), 1 apple (cored and chopped), ½ lemon (peeled and seeded), 1-inch piece of ginger (peeled), 1 cup cold water, 1 cup ice cubes

UK: 2 medium beetroots (peeled and chopped), 2 carrots (peeled and chopped), 1 apple (cored and chopped), ½ lemon (peeled and seeded), 2.5cm piece of ginger (peeled), 240ml cold water, 150g ice cubes

Instructions:
1. Place beetroots, carrots, apple, lemon, ginger, cold water, and ice cubes into the Ninja Foodi Cold & Hot Blender.
2. Select the "Juice" function and blend until vibrant and smooth.
3. Pour into glasses and enjoy the earthy sweetness of this ruby-red juice.

Nutritional Info: Calories: 90 | Fat: 0g | Carbs: 22g | Protein: 2g

Spicy Tomato Recovery

Prep: 5 mins | Serves: 2
Ingredients:

US: 3 large tomatoes (quartered), 1 celery stalk (chopped), ½ cucumber (chopped), ½ red bell pepper (chopped), 1 small chilli pepper (seeded), ½ lemon (peeled and seeded), 1 cup cold water, 1 cup ice cubes

UK: 3 large tomatoes (quartered), 1 celery stalk (chopped), ½ cucumber (chopped), ½ red bell pepper (chopped), 1 small chilli pepper (seeded), ½ lemon (peeled and seeded), 240ml cold water, 150g ice cubes

Instructions:
1. Add tomatoes, celery, cucumber, red bell pepper, chilli pepper, lemon, cold water, and ice cubes to the Ninja Foodi Cold & Hot Blender.
2. Choose the "Juice" function and blend until spicy and refreshing.
3. Pour into glasses and enjoy this invigorating and nutrient-packed recovery drink.

Nutritional Info: Calories: 45 | Fat: 0g | Carbs: 10g | Protein: 2g

Homemade Oat Milk

Prep: 10 mins | Serves: 4
Ingredients:
US: 1 cup rolled oats, 4 cups water, 1 teaspoon vanilla extract, 1 tablespoon maple syrup

UK: 150g rolled oats, 960ml water, 5ml vanilla extract, 15g maple syrup

Instructions:
1. Rinse rolled oats under cold water and drain.
2. Combine oats, water, vanilla extract, and maple syrup in the Ninja Foodi Cold & Hot Blender.
3. Select the "Nut Milk" function and blend until smooth.
4. Strain the mixture through a nut milk bag or fine sieve into a clean container.
5. Store in the refrigerator for up to 5 days and shake well before using.

Nutritional Info: Calories: 40 | Fat: 1g | Carbs: 7g | Protein: 1g

Golden Turmeric Latte

Prep: 5 mins | Cook: 5 mins | Serves: 2
Ingredients:
US: 2 cups milk (dairy or plant-based), 1 teaspoon ground turmeric, ½ teaspoon ground cinnamon, ¼ teaspoon ground ginger, 1 tablespoon honey or maple syrup, ½ teaspoon vanilla extract

UK: 480ml milk (dairy or plant-based), 5g ground turmeric, 2.5g ground cinnamon, 1.25g ground ginger, 15g honey or maple syrup, 2.5ml vanilla extract

Instructions:
1. In a small saucepan, heat the milk over medium heat until hot but not boiling.
2. Add ground turmeric, ground cinnamon, ground ginger, honey or maple syrup, and vanilla extract to the Ninja Foodi Cold & Hot Blender.
3. Pour the hot milk into the blender.
4. Secure the lid and select the "Soup" function. Blend until frothy and well combined.
5. Pour the turmeric latte into mugs and sprinkle with a pinch of ground cinnamon if desired. Serve immediately.

Nutritional Info: Calories: 150 | Fat: 5g | Carbs: 20g | Protein: 8g

Roasted Red Pepper Bisque

Prep: 10 mins | Cook: 20 mins | Serves: 4

Ingredients:

US: 4 large red bell peppers, 1 onion (chopped), 2 cloves garlic (minced), 2 tablespoons olive oil, 4 cups vegetable broth, 1 can (400g) diced tomatoes, 1 teaspoon smoked paprika, salt, pepper, fresh basil (for garnish)

UK: 4 large red bell peppers, 1 onion (chopped), 2 cloves garlic (minced), 30ml olive oil, 960ml vegetable broth, 1 can (400g) diced tomatoes, 5g smoked paprika, salt, pepper, fresh basil (for garnish)

Instructions:

1. Preheat your Ninja Foodi Cold & Hot Blender to the "Saute" function.
2. Add olive oil, chopped onion, and minced garlic. Saute until softened.
3. Add diced red bell peppers and continue to saute until they start to char.
4. Pour in vegetable broth, diced tomatoes, and smoked paprika. Season with salt and pepper.
5. Select the "Soup" function and cook until the peppers are tender and flavors are melded.
6. Once done, blend the soup until smooth using the "Blend" function.
7. Ladle into bowls, garnish with fresh basil, and serve hot.

Nutritional Info: Calories: 150 | Fat: 7g | Carbs: 20g | Protein: 4g

Thai Coconut Pumpkin Soup

Prep: 10 mins | Cook: 20 mins | Serves: 4

Ingredients:

US: 500g pumpkin (peeled and cubed), 1 onion (chopped), 2 cloves garlic (minced), 1 tablespoon red curry paste, 1 can (400ml) coconut milk, 4 cups vegetable broth, 1 tablespoon brown sugar, 1 tablespoon fish sauce (optional), salt, pepper, fresh coriander (for garnish)

UK: 500g pumpkin (peeled and cubed), 1 onion (chopped), 2 cloves garlic (minced), 15ml red curry paste, 1 can (400ml) coconut milk, 960ml vegetable broth, 15g brown sugar, 15ml fish sauce (optional), salt, pepper, fresh coriander (for garnish)

Instructions:

1. Place pumpkin, chopped onion, minced garlic, and red curry paste into the Ninja Foodi Cold & Hot Blender.
2. Add coconut milk, vegetable broth, brown sugar, and fish sauce (if using).
3. Select the "Soup" function and cook until the pumpkin is tender.
4. Once cooked, blend the soup until smooth using the "Blend" function.
5. Season with salt and pepper to taste.
6. Ladle into bowls, garnish with fresh coriander, and serve piping hot.

Nutritional Info: Calories: 220 | Fat: 17g | Carbs: 15g | Protein: 4g

Loaded Baked Potato Soup

Prep: 10 mins | Cook: 25 mins | Serves: 4

Ingredients:

US: 4 large potatoes (peeled and cubed), 1 onion (chopped), 2 cloves garlic (minced), 4 cups vegetable broth, 1 cup milk, 1 cup shredded cheddar cheese, 4 slices bacon (cooked and crumbled), salt, pepper, chopped chives (for garnish)

UK: 4 large potatoes (peeled and cubed), 1 onion (chopped), 2 cloves garlic (minced), 960ml vegetable broth, 240ml milk, 100g shredded cheddar cheese, 4 slices bacon (cooked and crumbled), salt, pepper, chopped chives (for garnish)

Instructions:

1. Place cubed potatoes, chopped onion, minced garlic, and vegetable broth into the Ninja Foodi Cold & Hot Blender.
2. Select the "Soup" function and cook until the potatoes are tender.
3. Once cooked, add milk and shredded cheddar cheese. Stir until the cheese is melted.

4. Season with salt and pepper to taste.
5. Ladle into bowls, top with crumbled bacon and chopped chives, and serve hot.

Nutritional Info: Calories: 350 | Fat: 15g | Carbs: 35g | Protein: 15g

Smoky Cheddar & Ale Soup

Prep: 10 mins | Cook: 25 mins | Serves: 4
Ingredients:

US: 2 tablespoons butter, 1 onion (chopped), 2 cloves garlic (minced), 2 tablespoons all-purpose flour, 2 cups vegetable broth, 1 cup ale beer, 2 cups shredded cheddar cheese, ½ teaspoon smoked paprika, salt, pepper, chopped chives (for garnish)

UK: 30g butter, 1 onion (chopped), 2 cloves garlic (minced), 30g all-purpose flour, 480ml vegetable broth, 240ml ale beer, 200g shredded cheddar cheese, 2.5g smoked paprika, salt, pepper, chopped chives (for garnish)

Instructions:
1. Preheat your Ninja Foodi Cold & Hot Blender to the "Saute" function.
2. Melt butter and saute chopped onion and minced garlic until softened.
3. Stir in all-purpose flour and cook until golden brown.
4. Gradually pour in vegetable broth and ale beer, stirring constantly.
5. Add shredded cheddar cheese and smoked paprika. Stir until the cheese is melted.
6. Season with salt and pepper to taste.
7. Ladle into bowls, garnish with chopped chives and serve with crusty bread.
8. Nutritional Info: Calories: 380 | Fat: 25g | Carbs: 15g | Protein: 15g

Curried Cauliflower Bisque

Prep: 10 mins | Cook: 25 mins | Serves: 4
Ingredients:

US: 1 head cauliflower (chopped), 1 onion (chopped), 2 cloves garlic (minced), 1 tablespoon curry powder, 4 cups vegetable broth, 1 can (400ml) coconut milk, salt, pepper, fresh coriander (for garnish)

UK: 1 head cauliflower (chopped), 1 onion (chopped), 2 cloves garlic (minced), 15ml curry powder, 960ml vegetable broth, 1 can (400ml) coconut milk, salt, pepper, fresh coriander (for garnish)

Instructions:

1. Place chopped cauliflower, chopped onion, minced garlic, and curry powder into the Ninja Foodi Cold & Hot Blender.
2. Add vegetable broth and coconut milk.
3. Select the "Soup" function and cook until the cauliflower is tender.
4. Once cooked, blend the soup until smooth using the "Blend" function.
5. Season with salt and pepper to taste.
6. Ladle into bowls, garnish with fresh coriander and serve hot.

Nutritional Info: Calories: 180 | Fat: 15g | Carbs: 10g | Protein: 4g

Chicken Enchilada Soup

Prep: 10 mins | Cook: 25 mins | Serves: 4

Ingredients:

US: 2 cups shredded cooked chicken, 1 onion (chopped), 2 cloves garlic (minced), 1 can (400g) diced tomatoes, 1 can (400g) black beans (drained and rinsed), 1 cup frozen corn kernels, 4 cups chicken broth, 1 tablespoon chilli powder, 1 teaspoon ground cumin, salt, pepper, shredded cheese (for garnish), chopped cilantro (for garnish)

UK: 300g shredded cooked chicken, 1 onion (chopped), 2 cloves garlic (minced), 1 can (400g) diced tomatoes, 1 can (400g) black beans (drained and rinsed), 150g frozen corn kernels, 960ml chicken broth, 15ml chilli powder, 5ml ground cumin, salt, pepper, shredded cheese (for garnish), chopped cilantro (for garnish)

Instructions:

1. Place shredded cooked chicken, chopped onion, minced garlic, diced tomatoes, black beans, frozen corn kernels, chicken broth, chilli powder, and ground cumin into the Ninja Foodi Cold & Hot Blender.
2. Select the "Soup" function and cook until heated through.
3. Season with salt and pepper to taste.
4. Ladle into bowls, top with shredded cheese and chopped cilantro, and serve hot.

Nutritional Info: Calories: 300 | Fat: 7g | Carbs: 25g | Protein: 30g

Chilled Cucumber Gazpacho

Prep: 10 mins (+chilling time) | Serves: 4

Ingredients:

US: 2 large cucumbers (peeled and chopped), 1 green bell pepper (chopped), 1 onion (chopped), 2 cloves garlic (minced), 2 cups vegetable broth, ½ cup Greek yogurt, 2 tablespoons lemon juice, 2 tablespoons olive oil, salt, pepper, fresh dill (for garnish)

UK: 2 large cucumbers (peeled and chopped), 1 green bell pepper (chopped), 1 onion (chopped), 2 cloves garlic (minced), 480ml vegetable broth, 120g Greek yogurt, 30ml lemon juice, 30ml olive oil, salt, pepper, fresh dill (for garnish)

Instructions:

1. Place chopped cucumbers, chopped green bell pepper, chopped onion, minced garlic, vegetable broth, Greek yogurt, lemon juice, and olive oil into the Ninja Foodi Cold & Hot Blender.
2. Select the "Soup" function and blend until smooth.
3. Season with salt and pepper to taste.
4. Transfer the gazpacho to a bowl, cover, and chill in the refrigerator for at least 1 hour.
5. Before serving, garnish with fresh dill and a drizzle of olive oil.

Nutritional Info: Calories: 120 | Fat: 8g | Carbs: 10g | Protein: 4g

Harvest Vegetable Soup

Prep: 10 mins | Cook: 25 mins | Serves: 4

Ingredients:

US: 1 onion (chopped), 2 carrots (peeled and chopped), 2 celery stalks (chopped), 1 sweet potato (peeled and chopped), 4 cups vegetable broth, 1 can (400g) diced tomatoes, 1 cup chopped kale leaves, 1 teaspoon dried thyme, salt, pepper, grated Parmesan cheese (for garnish)

UK: 1 onion (chopped), 2 carrots (peeled and chopped), 2 celery stalks (chopped), 1 sweet potato (peeled and chopped), 960ml vegetable broth, 1 can (400g) diced tomatoes, 100g chopped kale leaves, 5g dried thyme, salt, pepper, grated Parmesan cheese (for garnish)

Instructions:

1. Place chopped onion, carrots, celery, sweet potato, vegetable broth, diced tomatoes, chopped kale leaves, and dried thyme into the Ninja Foodi Cold & Hot Blender.
2. Select the "Soup" function and cook until the vegetables are tender.
3. Season with salt and pepper to taste.

4. Ladle into bowls, sprinkle with grated Parmesan cheese and serve hot.

Nutritional Info: Calories: 150 | Fat: 2g | Carbs: 30g | Protein: 6g

Spicy Black Bean Soup

Prep: 10 mins | Cook: 25 mins | Serves: 4
Ingredients:

US: 2 cans (400g each) black beans (drained and rinsed), 1 onion (chopped), 2 cloves garlic (minced), 1 red bell pepper (chopped), 1 can (400g) diced tomatoes, 4 cups vegetable broth, 1 tablespoon chilli powder, 1 teaspoon ground cumin, salt, pepper, sour cream (for garnish), chopped cilantro (for garnish)

UK: 2 cans (400g each) black beans (drained and rinsed), 1 onion (chopped), 2 cloves garlic (minced), 1 red bell pepper (chopped), 1 can (400g) diced tomatoes, 960ml vegetable broth, 15ml chilli powder, 5ml ground cumin, salt, pepper, sour cream (for garnish), chopped cilantro (for garnish)

Instructions:

1. Place black beans, chopped onion, minced garlic, chopped red bell pepper, diced tomatoes, vegetable broth, chilli powder, and ground cumin into the Ninja Foodi Cold & Hot Blender.
2. Select the "Soup" function and cook until heated through.
3. Season with salt and pepper to taste.
4. Ladle into bowls, top with a dollop of sour cream and chopped cilantro, and serve hot.

Nutritional Info: Calories: 280 | Fat: 2g | Carbs: 50g | Protein: 15g

Broccoli Cheddar Soup

Prep: 10 mins | Cook: 25 mins | Serves: 4
Ingredients:

US: 2 cups chopped broccoli florets, 1 onion (chopped), 2 cloves garlic (minced), 4 cups vegetable broth, 1 cup milk, 2 cups shredded cheddar cheese, 2 tablespoons all-purpose flour, salt, pepper, chopped chives (for garnish)

UK: 300g chopped broccoli florets, 1 onion (chopped), 2 cloves garlic (minced), 960ml vegetable broth, 240ml milk, 200g shredded cheddar cheese, 30g all-purpose flour, salt, pepper, chopped chives (for garnish)

Instructions:

1. Place chopped broccoli florets, chopped onion, minced garlic, and vegetable broth into the Ninja Foodi Cold & Hot Blender.
2. Select the "Soup" function and cook until the broccoli is tender.
3. In a separate saucepan, whisk together milk and all-purpose flour until smooth. Heat over medium heat until thickened.
4. Add shredded cheddar cheese to the thickened milk mixture and stir until melted.
5. Pour the cheese mixture into the blender with the cooked broccoli.
6. Select the "Blend" function and blend until smooth.
7. Season with salt and pepper to taste.
8. Ladle into bowls, garnish with chopped chives and serve hot.

Nutritional Info: Calories: 350 | Fat: 20g | Carbs: 20g | Protein: 15g

Roasted Garlic Hummus

Prep: 10 mins | Cook: 30 mins | Serves: 6
Ingredients:

US: 2 cans (400g each) chickpeas (drained and rinsed), 1 bulb garlic, 60ml olive oil, 3 tablespoons tahini, 3 tablespoons lemon juice, 1 teaspoon ground cumin, salt, pepper, paprika (for garnish)

UK: 2 cans (400g each) chickpeas (drained and rinsed), 1 bulb garlic, 60ml olive oil, 3 tablespoons tahini, 3 tablespoons lemon juice, 5g ground cumin, salt, pepper, paprika (for garnish)

Instructions:

1. Preheat your Ninja Foodi Cold & Hot Blender to the "Roast" function.
2. Slice the top off the garlic bulb to expose the cloves. Drizzle with olive oil, wrap in foil, and roast for 30 minutes.
3. Once roasted, squeeze the softened garlic cloves out of their skins into the blender.
4. Add drained chickpeas, tahini, lemon juice, ground cumin, salt, and pepper to the blender.
5. Select the "Blend" function and blend until smooth.
6. Adjust seasoning if necessary and transfer to a serving bowl.
7. Drizzle with olive oil, sprinkle with paprika, and serve with your favorite dippers.

Nutritional Info: Calories: 200 | Fat: 10g | Carbs: 20g | Protein: 8g

Charred Corn Salsa

Prep: 10 mins | Cook: 10 mins | Serves: 4
Ingredients:

US: 2 cups corn kernels (fresh or frozen), 1 red onion (diced), 1 jalapeno (seeded and diced), 1 red bell pepper (diced), 1 tomato (diced), 2 tablespoons lime juice, 2 tablespoons chopped fresh cilantro, salt, pepper

UK: 300g corn kernels (fresh or frozen), 1 red onion (diced), 1 jalapeno (seeded and diced), 1 red bell pepper (diced), 1 tomato (diced), 30ml lime juice, 30ml chopped fresh cilantro, salt, pepper

Instructions:

1. Preheat your Ninja Foodi Cold & Hot Blender to the "Grill" function.
2. Place corn kernels, diced red onion, diced jalapeno, and diced red bell pepper on the grill and char for about 10 minutes, stirring occasionally.
3. Once charred, transfer the grilled ingredients to the blender.

4. Add diced tomato, lime juice, chopped cilantro, salt, and pepper to the blender.
5. Select the "Chop" function and pulse until desired consistency is reached.
6. Taste and adjust seasoning if needed.
7. Transfer to a serving bowl and serve with tortilla chips or as a topping for grilled meats.

Nutritional Info: Calories: 100 | Fat: 1g | Carbs: 25g | Protein: 3g

Baba Ghanoush

Prep: 10 mins | Cook: 30 mins | Serves: 6
Ingredients:

US: 2 large eggplants, 2 cloves garlic (minced), 3 tablespoons tahini, 2 tablespoons lemon juice, 2 tablespoons olive oil, salt, pepper, chopped fresh parsley (for garnish)

UK: 2 large eggplants, 2 cloves garlic (minced), 3 tablespoons tahini, 2 tablespoons lemon juice, 30ml olive oil, salt, pepper, chopped fresh parsley (for garnish)

Instructions:
1. Preheat your Ninja Foodi Cold & Hot Blender to the "Roast" function.
2. Pierce the eggplants with a fork and place them directly on the grill. Roast for 30 minutes, turning occasionally, until charred and soft.
3. Once roasted, remove the eggplants from the grill and let them cool slightly.
4. Peel off the charred skin and discard.
5. Place the roasted eggplant flesh, minced garlic, tahini, lemon juice, and olive oil into the blender.
6. Select the "Blend" function and blend until smooth.
7. Season with salt and pepper to taste.
8. Transfer to a serving bowl, drizzle with olive oil, sprinkle with chopped parsley, and serve with pita bread or veggies.

Nutritional Info: Calories: 150 | Fat: 10g | Carbs: 15g | Protein: 3g

Cashew Sour Cream

Prep: 5 mins (+ soaking time) | Serves: 8
Ingredients:

US: 1 cup raw cashews (soaked in water for 4 hours), ½ cup water, 2 tablespoons lemon juice, 1 tablespoon apple cider vinegar, salt

UK: 150g raw cashews (soaked in water for 4 hours), 120ml water, 30ml lemon juice, 15ml apple cider vinegar, salt

Instructions:

1. Drain soaked cashews and rinse under cold water.
2. Place soaked cashews, water, lemon juice, apple cider vinegar, and a pinch of salt into the blender.
3. Select the "Blend" function and blend until smooth and creamy.
4. Taste and adjust seasoning if necessary.
5. Transfer to a jar or container and refrigerate until ready to use.
6. Use as a dairy-free alternative to sour cream on tacos, nachos, or baked potatoes.

Nutritional Info: Calories: 60 | Fat: 5g | Carbs: 3g | Protein: 2g

Chipotle Romesco

Prep: 10 mins | Cook: 10 mins | Serves: 6

Ingredients:

US: 1 cup roasted red peppers, ½ cup almonds (toasted), 2 cloves garlic, 2 tablespoons tomato paste, 1 tablespoon chipotle peppers in adobo sauce, 2 tablespoons red wine vinegar, 2 tablespoons olive oil, salt, pepper

UK: 240ml roasted red peppers, 60g almonds (toasted), 2 cloves garlic, 30ml tomato paste, 15ml chipotle peppers in adobo sauce, 30ml red wine vinegar, 30ml olive oil, salt, pepper

Instructions:

1. Place roasted red peppers, toasted almonds, garlic cloves, tomato paste, chipotle peppers in adobo sauce, red wine vinegar, and olive oil into the blender.
2. Select the "Blend" function and blend until smooth.
3. Season with salt and pepper to taste.
4. Transfer to a serving bowl or jar and refrigerate until ready to use.
5. Serve as a dip for crudites, a spread for sandwiches, or a sauce for grilled meats.

Nutritional Info: Calories: 120 | Fat: 10g | Carbs: 5g | Protein: 3g

Green Goddess Dressing

Prep: 5 mins | Serves: 8
Ingredients:

US: 1 avocado, ½ cup Greek yoghurt, 1 clove garlic, 2 tablespoons lemon juice, 2 tablespoons chopped fresh parsley, 2 tablespoons chopped fresh basil, 1 tablespoon chopped fresh chives, salt, pepper

UK: 1 avocado, 120ml Greek yoghurt, 1 clove garlic, 30ml lemon juice, 30ml chopped fresh parsley, 30ml chopped fresh basil, 15ml chopped fresh chives, salt, pepper

Instructions:
1. Scoop the flesh of the avocado into the blender.
2. Add Greek yoghurt, garlic clove, lemon juice, chopped parsley, chopped basil, and chopped chives to the blender.
3. Select the "Blend" function and blend until smooth and creamy.
4. Season with salt and pepper to taste.
5. Transfer to a jar or container and refrigerate until ready to use.
6. Serve as a dressing for salads, a dip for veggies, or a spread for sandwiches.

Nutritional Info: Calories: 50 | Fat: 4g | Carbs: 3g | Protein: 2g

Satay Peanut Sauce

Prep: 5 mins | Cook: 5 mins | Serves: 6
Ingredients:

US: ½ cup creamy peanut butter, ¼ cup coconut milk, 2 tablespoons soy sauce, 2 tablespoons lime juice, 1 tablespoon honey, 1 clove garlic (minced), 1 teaspoon grated ginger, salt, pepper, water (as needed)

UK: 120ml creamy peanut butter, 60ml coconut milk, 30ml soy sauce, 30ml lime juice, 15ml honey, 1 clove garlic (minced), 5ml grated ginger, salt, pepper, water (as needed)

Instructions:
1. Place creamy peanut butter, coconut milk, soy sauce, lime juice, honey, minced garlic, and grated ginger into the blender.
2. Select the "Blend" function and blend until smooth.
3. If the sauce is too thick, add water a little at a time until desired consistency is reached.
4. Season with salt and pepper to taste.
5. Transfer to a serving bowl or jar and refrigerate until ready to use.

6. Serve as a dipping sauce for satay skewers, spring rolls, or grilled meats.

Nutritional Info: Calories: 150 | Fat: 12g | Carbs: 8g | Protein: 5g

Zhoug Herb Relish

Prep: 10 mins | Serves: 8
Ingredients:

US: 2 cups fresh cilantro, 1 cup fresh parsley, 2 cloves garlic, 1 jalapeno (seeded), 1 teaspoon ground cumin, ½ teaspoon ground cardamom, ½ teaspoon salt, ¼ teaspoon black pepper, ¼ cup olive oil, 2 tablespoons lemon juice

UK: 480ml fresh cilantro, 240ml fresh parsley, 2 cloves garlic, 1 jalapeno (seeded), 5ml ground cumin, 2.5ml ground cardamom, 2.5ml salt, 1.25ml black pepper, 60ml olive oil, 30ml lemon juice

Instructions:

1. Place fresh cilantro, fresh parsley, garlic cloves, seeded jalapeno, ground cumin, ground cardamom, salt, black pepper, olive oil, and lemon juice into the blender.
2. Select the "Blend" function and blend until finely chopped and well combined.
3. Taste and adjust seasoning if necessary.
4. Transfer to a jar or container and refrigerate until ready to use.
5. Serve as a condiment for grilled meats, roasted vegetables, or as a spread for sandwiches.

Nutritional Info: Calories: 60 | Fat: 6g | Carbs: 2g | Protein: 1g

Smoky Pecan Butter

Prep: 5 mins | Cook: 10 mins | Serves: 8
Ingredients:

US: 2 cups pecans, 1 tablespoon maple syrup, ½ teaspoon smoked paprika, ¼ teaspoon cayenne pepper, salt

UK: 240ml pecans, 15ml maple syrup, 2.5ml smoked paprika, 1.25ml cayenne pepper, salt

Instructions:

1. Preheat your Ninja Foodi Cold & Hot Blender to the "Roast" function.
2. Place pecans on the grill and roast for 10 minutes, stirring occasionally, until fragrant and toasted.
3. Transfer the roasted pecans to the blender.
4. Add maple syrup, smoked paprika, cayenne pepper, and a pinch of salt to the blender.
5. Select the "Blend" function and blend until smooth and creamy.

6. Taste and adjust seasoning if necessary.
7. Transfer to a jar or container and refrigerate until ready to use.
8. Enjoy as a spread on toast, a dip for apple slices, or a topping for oatmeal.

Nutritional Info: Calories: 200 | Fat: 20g | Carbs: 5g | Protein: 3g

Preserved Lemon Dressing

Prep: 5 mins | Serves: 8
Ingredients:

US: 1 preserved lemon, ½ cup olive oil, 2 tablespoons lemon juice, 1 teaspoon honey, salt, pepper

UK: 1 preserved lemon, 120ml olive oil, 30ml lemon juice, 5ml honey, salt, pepper

Instructions:

1. Rinse the preserved lemon under cold water to remove excess salt.
2. Cut the preserved lemon into quarters and remove the seeds.
3. Place preserved lemon, olive oil, lemon juice, honey, salt, and pepper into the blender.
4. Select the "Blend" function and blend until smooth.
5. Taste and adjust seasoning if necessary.
6. Transfer to a jar or container and refrigerate until ready to use.
7. Serve as a dressing for salads, a marinade for grilled meats, or a sauce for roasted vegetables.

Nutritional Info: Calories: 120 | Fat: 14g | Carbs: 2g | Protein: 1g

Chapter 5: Frozen Treats

Peanut Butter Banana "Nice" Cream

Prep: 5 mins | Cook: 0 mins | Serves: 2
Ingredients:

US: 2 ripe bananas (sliced and frozen), 2 tablespoons peanut butter, 60ml milk (or dairy-free alternative), 1 tablespoon honey (optional), chopped peanuts (for garnish)

UK: 2 ripe bananas (sliced and frozen), 30g peanut butter, 60ml milk (or dairy-free alternative), 15ml honey (optional), chopped peanuts (for garnish)

Instructions:
1. Place frozen banana slices, peanut butter, milk, and honey (if using) into the Ninja Foodi Cold & Hot Blender.
2. Select the "Blend" function and blend until smooth and creamy.
3. If necessary, stop and scrape down the sides of the blender to ensure all ingredients are incorporated.
4. Once creamy, scoop the "nice" cream into bowls.
5. Garnish with chopped peanuts.
6. Serve immediately for a deliciously creamy frozen treat!

Nutritional Info: Calories: 200 | Fat: 8g | Carbs: 30g | Protein: 5g

Raspberry Lime Sorbet

Prep: 5 mins (+ freezing time) | Cook: 0 mins | Serves: 4
Ingredients:

US: 300g frozen raspberries, 60ml lime juice, 60g sugar (or sweetener of choice), 120ml water

UK: 300g frozen raspberries, 60ml lime juice, 60g sugar (or sweetener of choice), 120ml water

Instructions:
1. In a saucepan, combine water and sugar. Heat over medium heat until sugar dissolves, then let it cool.
2. Place frozen raspberries, lime juice, and the cooled sugar syrup into the Ninja Foodi Cold & Hot Blender.
3. Select the "Blend" function and blend until smooth.
4. Pour the mixture into a shallow dish and freeze for at least 4 hours, stirring occasionally, until firm.

5. Once frozen, scoop the sorbet into bowls and serve immediately.
6. Enjoy the refreshing combination of tart raspberries and zesty lime!

Nutritional Info: Calories: 80 | Fat: 0g | Carbs: 20g | Protein: 1g

Nutella Milkshake

Prep: 5 mins | Cook: 0 mins | Serves: 2
Ingredients:

US: 2 cups vanilla ice cream, 4 tablespoons Nutella, 120ml milk, whipped cream (for topping), chocolate shavings (for garnish)

UK: 240ml vanilla ice cream, 60g Nutella, 120ml milk, whipped cream (for topping), chocolate shavings (for garnish)

Instructions:

1. Place vanilla ice cream, Nutella, and milk into the Ninja Foodi Cold & Hot Blender.
2. Select the "Blend" function and blend until smooth and creamy.
3. Pour the milkshake into glasses.
4. Top with whipped cream and chocolate shavings.
5. Serve immediately for a decadent and indulgent treat!

Nutritional Info: Calories: 400 | Fat: 20g | Carbs: 50g | Protein: 8g

Strawberry Daiquiri

Prep: 5 mins | Cook: 0 mins | Serves: 2
Ingredients:

US: 2 cups frozen strawberries, 120ml white rum, 60ml lime juice, 2 tablespoons simple syrup, ice cubes

UK: 240ml frozen strawberries, 120ml white rum, 60ml lime juice, 30ml simple syrup, ice cubes

Instructions:

1. Place frozen strawberries, white rum, lime juice, and simple syrup into the Ninja Foodi Cold & Hot Blender.
2. Add a handful of ice cubes to the blender.
3. Select the "Blend" function and blend until smooth.
4. Pour the daiquiri into glasses.
5. Garnish with a slice of lime or a strawberry, if desired.
6. Enjoy this classic cocktail in frozen form!

Nutritional Info: Calories: 150 | Fat: 0g | Carbs: 20g | Protein: 1g

Coconut Mango Freeze

Prep: 5 mins | Cook: 0 mins | Serves: 2
Ingredients:

US: 1 cup frozen mango chunks, 120ml coconut milk, 60ml pineapple juice, 1 tablespoon honey (optional), shredded coconut (for garnish)

UK: 150g frozen mango chunks, 120ml coconut milk, 60ml pineapple juice, 15ml honey (optional), shredded coconut (for garnish)

Instructions:
1. Place frozen mango chunks, coconut milk, pineapple juice, and honey (if using) into the Ninja Foodi Cold & Hot Blender.
2. Select the "Blend" function and blend until smooth.
3. Pour the mango freeze into glasses.
4. Garnish with shredded coconut.
5. Serve immediately for a tropical delight!

Nutritional Info: Calories: 200 | Fat: 10g | Carbs: 30g | Protein: 1g

Black Forest Shake

Prep: 5 mins | Cook: 0 mins | Serves: 2
Ingredients:

US: 2 cups chocolate ice cream, 120ml cherry juice, 60ml milk, whipped cream (for topping), maraschino cherries (for garnish)

UK: 240ml chocolate ice cream, 120ml cherry juice, 60ml milk, whipped cream (for topping), maraschino cherries (for garnish)

Instructions:
1. Place chocolate ice cream, cherry juice, and milk into the Ninja Foodi Cold & Hot Blender.
2. Select the "Blend" function and blend until smooth and creamy.
3. Pour the shake into the glasses.
4. Top with whipped cream and a maraschino cherry.
5. Indulge in this decadent twist on the classic Black Forest dessert!

Nutritional Info: Calories: 400 | Fat: 20g | Carbs: 50g | Protein: 8g

Oreo Milkshake

Prep: 5 mins | Cook: 0 mins | Serves: 2
Ingredients:

US: 2 cups vanilla ice cream, 4 Oreo cookies, 120ml milk, whipped cream (for topping), crushed Oreo cookies (for garnish)

UK: 240ml vanilla ice cream, 4 Oreo cookies, 120ml milk, whipped cream (for topping), crushed Oreo cookies (for garnish)

Instructions:

1. Place vanilla ice cream, Oreo cookies, and milk into the Ninja Foodi Cold & Hot Blender.
2. Select the "Blend" function and blend until smooth and creamy.
3. Pour the milkshake into glasses.
4. Top with whipped cream and crushed Oreo cookies.
5. Enjoy the irresistible combination of creamy vanilla, chocolate, and cookie goodness!

Nutritional Info: Calories: 400 | Fat: 20g | Carbs: 50g | Protein: 8g

Watermelon Margarita Slushie

Prep: 5 mins | Cook: 0 mins | Serves: 2
Ingredients:

US: 2 cups frozen watermelon cubes, 120ml tequila, 60ml triple sec, 60ml lime juice, 2 tablespoons agave syrup (optional), lime wedges (for garnish), salt (for rimming, optional)

UK: 240ml frozen watermelon cubes, 120ml tequila, 60ml triple sec, 60ml lime juice, 30ml agave syrup (optional), lime wedges (for garnish), salt (for rimming, optional)

Instructions:

1. Place frozen watermelon cubes, tequila, triple sec, lime juice, and agave syrup (if using) into the Ninja Foodi Cold & Hot Blender.
2. Select the "Blend" function and blend until smooth and slushy.
3. If desired, rim glasses with salt by running a lime wedge around the rim and dipping it in salt.
4. Pour the slushie into glasses.
5. Garnish with lime wedges.
6. Enjoy this refreshing and boozy twist on a classic summer treat!

Nutritional Info: Calories: 200 | Fat: 0g | Carbs: 30g | Protein: 1g

Mint Choc Chip "Nice" Cream

Prep: 5 mins (+ freezing time) | Cook: 0 mins | Serves: 2
Ingredients:

US: 2 ripe bananas (sliced and frozen), 2 tablespoons maple syrup, ½ teaspoon peppermint extract, 30g dark chocolate (chopped), fresh mint leaves (for garnish)

UK: 2 ripe bananas (sliced and frozen), 30ml maple syrup, 2.5ml peppermint extract, 30g dark chocolate (chopped), fresh mint leaves (for garnish)

Instructions:

1. Place frozen banana slices, maple syrup, and peppermint extract into the Ninja Foodi Cold & Hot Blender.
2. Select the "Blend" function and blend until smooth and creamy.
3. Add chopped dark chocolate to the blender and pulse a few times to incorporate.
4. Transfer the mint choc chip "nice" cream into a shallow dish and freeze for at least 2 hours until firm.
5. Once frozen, scoop the "nice" cream into bowls.
6. Garnish with fresh mint leaves.
7. Enjoy this guilt-free and refreshing frozen treat!

Nutritional Info: Calories: 200 | Fat: 5g | Carbs: 40g | Protein: 2g

Boozy Mudslide

Prep: 5 mins | Cook: 0 mins | Serves: 2
Ingredients:

US: 2 cups vanilla ice cream, 60ml vodka, 60ml coffee liqueur, 60ml Irish cream liqueur, whipped cream (for topping), chocolate syrup (for garnish)

UK: 240ml vanilla ice cream, 60ml vodka, 60ml coffee liqueur, 60ml Irish cream liqueur, whipped cream (for topping), chocolate syrup (for garnish)

Instructions:

1. Place vanilla ice cream, vodka, coffee liqueur, and Irish cream liqueur into the Ninja Foodi Cold & Hot Blender.
2. Select the "Blend" function and blend until smooth and creamy.
3. Pour the mudslide into glasses.
4. Top with whipped cream and a drizzle of chocolate syrup.
5. Indulge in this decadent and boozy dessert cocktail!

Nutritional Info: Calories: 500 | Fat: 20g | Carbs: 50g | Protein: 6g

Chapter 6: Baby Food Purees

Sweet Potato & Apple Mash

Prep: 10 mins | Cook: 15 mins | Serves: 4
Ingredients:

US: 300g sweet potatoes (peeled and diced), 200g apples (peeled, cored, and diced), water (for boiling)

UK: 300g sweet potatoes (peeled and diced), 200g apples (peeled, cored, and diced), water (for boiling)

Instructions:

1. Place diced sweet potatoes and apples into a pot and cover with water.
2. Bring to a boil and simmer for about 10-15 minutes until both are tender.
3. Drain the water and transfer the cooked sweet potatoes and apples to the Ninja Foodi Cold & Hot Blender.
4. Select the "Puree" function and blend until smooth.
5. If necessary, add a little water or breast milk to achieve the desired consistency.
6. Serve warm or at room temperature.
7. Store any leftovers in an airtight container in the refrigerator for up to 3 days.

Nutritional Info: Calories: 80 | Fat: 0g | Carbs: 20g | Protein: 1g

Pear & Spinach Blend

Prep: 10 mins | Cook: 0 mins | Serves: 4
Ingredients:

US: 300g pears (peeled, cored, and chopped), 100g spinach leaves, water (as needed)

UK: 300g pears (peeled, cored, and chopped), 100g spinach leaves, water (as needed)

Instructions:

1. Place chopped pears and spinach leaves into the Ninja Foodi Cold & Hot Blender.
2. Add a little water if needed to help with blending.
3. Select the "Puree" function and blend until smooth.
4. Check the consistency and add more water if necessary.
5. Transfer the pear and spinach blend into serving bowls.
6. Serve immediately or refrigerate for later use.
7. Ensure the puree is at a suitable temperature before feeding to your baby.

Nutritional Info: Calories: 50 | Fat: 0g | Carbs: 15g | Protein: 1g

Banana & Blueberry Oat Mash

Prep: 5 mins | Cook: 5 mins | Serves: 4

Ingredients:

US: 2 ripe bananas, 100g blueberries, 30g rolled oats, water (as needed)

UK: 2 ripe bananas, 100g blueberries, 30g rolled oats, water (as needed)

Instructions:

1. In a small saucepan, combine the bananas, blueberries, and rolled oats.
2. Add enough water to cover the ingredients.
3. Cook over medium heat for about 5 minutes, stirring occasionally, until the fruits are soft and the oats are cooked.
4. Allow the mixture to cool slightly.
5. Transfer the mixture to the Ninja Foodi Cold & Hot Blender.
6. Select the "Puree" function and blend until smooth.
7. Add more water if necessary to reach the desired consistency.
8. Serve warm or refrigerate for later use.
9. Ensure the temperature is suitable for your baby before serving.

Nutritional Info: Calories: 60 | Fat: 0g | Carbs: 15g | Protein: 1g

Butternut & White Bean Puree

Prep: 10 mins | Cook: 20 mins | Serves: 4

Ingredients:

US: 300g butternut squash (peeled, seeded, and cubed), 200g canned white beans (drained and rinsed), vegetable broth (as needed)

UK: 300g butternut squash (peeled, seeded, and cubed), 200g canned white beans (drained and rinsed), vegetable broth (as needed)

Instructions:

1. Steam the cubed butternut squash until tender, about 15-20 minutes.
2. In a blender, combine the cooked butternut squash and white beans.
3. Add vegetable broth as needed to achieve a smooth consistency.
4. Blend until smooth using the "Puree" function on the Ninja Foodi Cold & Hot Blender.
5. Check the consistency and adjust with more vegetable broth if necessary.

6. Serve warm or at room temperature.
7. Store any leftovers in the refrigerator for up to 3 days.

Nutritional Info: Calories: 70 | Fat: 0g | Carbs: 15g | Protein: 3g

Mango & Greek Yogurt Puree

Prep: 5 mins | Cook: 0 mins | Serves: 4
Ingredients:

US: 300g ripe mango (peeled and chopped), 120g Greek yoghurt, water (as needed)

UK: 300g ripe mango (peeled and chopped), 120g Greek yoghurt, water (as needed)

Instructions:
1. Place chopped mango and Greek yoghurt into the Ninja Foodi Cold & Hot Blender.
2. Add a little water if needed to facilitate blending.
3. Select the "Puree" function and blend until smooth.
4. Check the consistency and add more water if necessary.
5. Transfer the puree into serving bowls.
6. Serve immediately or refrigerate for later use.
7. Ensure the puree is at an appropriate temperature before serving to your baby.

Nutritional Info: Calories: 80 | Fat: 0g | Carbs: 20g | Protein: 3g

Carrot & Cheddar Mash

Prep: 10 mins | Cook: 15 mins | Serves: 4
Ingredients:

US: 300g carrots (peeled and chopped), 60g cheddar cheese (grated), water (for boiling)

UK: 300g carrots (peeled and chopped), 60g cheddar cheese (grated), water (for boiling)

Instructions:
1. Steam or boil the chopped carrots until tender, about 10-15 minutes.
2. Drain the carrots and transfer them to the Ninja Foodi Cold & Hot Blender.
3. Add grated cheddar cheese to the blender.
4. Select the "Puree" function and blend until smooth.
5. If necessary, add a little water to achieve the desired consistency.
6. Serve warm or at room temperature.
7. Store any leftover mash in the refrigerator for up to 3 days.

Nutritional Info: Calories: 90 | Fat: 5g | Carbs: 10g | Protein: 4g

Cinnamon Pumpkin Puree

Prep: 10 mins | Cook: 20 mins | Serves: 4
Ingredients:

US: 300g pumpkin (peeled and cubed), ½ teaspoon ground cinnamon, water (for boiling)

UK: 300g pumpkin (peeled and cubed), ½ teaspoon ground cinnamon, water (for boiling)

Instructions:

1. Boil or steam the cubed pumpkin until soft, about 15-20 minutes.
2. Drain the pumpkin and transfer it to the Ninja Foodi Cold & Hot Blender.
3. Add ground cinnamon to the blender.
4. Select the "Puree" function and blend until smooth.
5. Adjust the consistency with water if needed.
6. Serve warm or at room temperature.
7. Store any remaining puree in the refrigerator for up to 3 days.

Nutritional Info: Calories: 50 | Fat: 0g | Carbs: 12g | Protein: 1g

Beetroot & Orange Puree

Prep: 10 mins | Cook: 30 mins | Serves: 4
Ingredients:

US: 300g beetroot (peeled and diced), juice of 1 orange, water (for boiling)

UK: 300g beetroot (peeled and diced), juice of 1 orange, water (for boiling)

Instructions:

1. Boil or steam the diced beetroot until tender, about 20-30 minutes.
2. Drain the beetroot and place it in the Ninja Foodi Cold & Hot Blender.
3. Add freshly squeezed orange juice to the blender.
4. Select the "Puree" function and blend until smooth.
5. Adjust the consistency with water if necessary.
6. Serve warm or at room temperature.
7. Store any leftover puree in the refrigerator for up to 3 days.

Nutritional Info: Calories: 60 | Fat: 0g | Carbs: 15g | Protein: 2g

Avocado & Pea Mash

Prep: 5 mins | Cook: 0 mins | Serves: 4
Ingredients:

US: 1 ripe avocado, 200g frozen peas (thawed), lemon juice (optional)

UK: 1 ripe avocado, 200g frozen peas (thawed), lemon juice (optional)

Instructions:
1. Scoop the flesh of the avocado into the Ninja Foodi Cold & Hot Blender.
2. Add the thawed peas to the blender.
3. Optionally, add a splash of lemon juice for extra flavor.
4. Select the "Puree" function and blend until smooth.
5. If needed, add a little water to achieve the desired consistency.
6. Serve immediately or refrigerate for later use.
7. Ensure the temperature is suitable for your baby before serving.

Nutritional Info: Calories: 100 | Fat: 7g | Carbs: 8g | Protein: 3g

Tropical Fruit Blend

Prep: 10 mins | Cook: 0 mins | Serves: 4
Ingredients:

US: 200g pineapple chunks, 200g mango chunks, 200g papaya chunks, water (as needed)

UK: 200g pineapple chunks, 200g mango chunks, 200g papaya chunks, water (as needed)

Instructions:
1. Place pineapple chunks, mango chunks, and papaya chunks into the Ninja Foodi Cold & Hot Blender.
2. Add a little water if needed to aid blending.
3. Select the "Puree" function and blend until smooth.
4. Check the consistency and add more water if required.
5. Serve immediately or store in the refrigerator for later use.
6. Ensure the puree is at a suitable temperature before feeding your baby.

Nutritional Info: Calories: 80 | Fat: 0g | Carbs: 20g | Protein: 1g

Chapter 7: Blender Baking

Banana Bread Batter

Prep: 10 mins | Cook: 50 mins | Serves: 1 loaf
Ingredients:

US: 3 ripe bananas, 120g sugar, 60ml vegetable oil, 2 eggs, 1 teaspoon vanilla extract, 180g all-purpose flour, 1 teaspoon baking soda, ½ teaspoon salt

UK: 3 ripe bananas, 120g sugar, 60ml vegetable oil, 2 eggs, 1 teaspoon vanilla extract, 180g all-purpose flour, 1 teaspoon baking soda, ½ teaspoon salt

Instructions:
1. Preheat your oven to 350°F (180°C) and grease a loaf pan.
2. In the Ninja Foodi Cold & Hot Blender, combine bananas, sugar, vegetable oil, eggs, and vanilla extract.
3. Blend on the "Mix" function until smooth.
4. Add flour, baking soda, and salt to the blender.
5. Blend on the "Mix" function until just combined.
6. Pour the batter into the prepared loaf pan.
7. Bake for 50-60 minutes or until a toothpick inserted into the centre comes out clean.
8. Allow the banana bread to cool in the pan for 10 minutes before transferring it to a wire rack to cool completely.
9. Slice and serve!

Nutritional Info: Calories: 250 | Fat: 8g | Carbs: 40g | Protein: 4g

Fluffy Pancake Mix

Prep: 5 mins | Cook: 10 mins | Serves: 4
Ingredients:

US: 200g all-purpose flour, 2 tablespoons sugar, 2 teaspoons baking powder, ½ teaspoon salt, 240ml milk, 2 tablespoons melted butter, 1 egg

UK: 200g all-purpose flour, 2 tablespoons sugar, 2 teaspoons baking powder, ½ teaspoon salt, 240ml milk, 2 tablespoons melted butter, 1 egg

Instructions:
1. In the Ninja Foodi Cold & Hot Blender, combine flour, sugar, baking powder, and salt.
2. Blend on the "Mix" function until well combined.

3. Add milk, melted butter, and egg to the blender.
4. Blend on the "Mix" function until smooth.
5. Heat a non-stick pan over medium heat and lightly grease with butter or oil.
6. Pour the pancake batter onto the pan to form circles.
7. Cook for 2-3 minutes until bubbles form on the surface, then flip and cook for another 1-2 minutes until golden brown.
8. Repeat with the remaining batter.
9. Serve warm with your favourite toppings!

Nutritional Info: Calories: 200 | Fat: 6g | Carbs: 30g | Protein: 6g

Herb & Garlic Pizza Dough

Prep: 15 mins | Cook: 15 mins | Serves: 2 pizzas
Ingredients:

US: 300g all-purpose flour, 1 teaspoon sugar, 1 teaspoon salt, 1 tablespoon dried herbs (such as oregano, basil, thyme), 2 cloves garlic (minced), 1 tablespoon olive oil, 1 teaspoon instant yeast, 180ml warm water

UK: 300g all-purpose flour, 1 teaspoon sugar, 1 teaspoon salt, 1 tablespoon dried herbs (such as oregano, basil, thyme), 2 cloves garlic (minced), 1 tablespoon olive oil, 1 teaspoon instant yeast, 180ml warm water

Instructions:
1. In the Ninja Foodi Cold & Hot Blender, combine flour, sugar, salt, dried herbs, minced garlic, olive oil, and instant yeast.
2. Blend on the "Dough" function until a dough forms.
3. Slowly add warm water while blending until the dough comes together and pulls away from the sides.
4. Transfer the dough to a lightly floured surface and knead for a few minutes until smooth.
5. Divide the dough into two equal portions and shape each into a ball.
6. Place the dough balls in greased bowls, cover them with a clean kitchen towel, and let them rise in a warm place for about 1 hour or until doubled in size.
7. Preheat your oven to the highest temperature setting.
8. Roll out the dough on a floured surface to your desired thickness.
9. Top with your favourite pizza toppings and bake for 10-15 minutes or until the crust is golden brown and crispy.
10. Slice and enjoy your homemade pizza!

Nutritional Info: (Dough only) Calories: 300 | Fat: 4g | Carbs: 55g | Protein: 8g

Peanut Butter Cookie Dough

Prep: 10 mins | Cook: 10 mins | Serves: 24 cookies

Ingredients:

US: 200g all-purpose flour, ½ teaspoon baking soda, ½ teaspoon salt, 120g unsalted butter (softened), 100g granulated sugar, 100g brown sugar, 1 teaspoon vanilla extract, 125g smooth peanut butter, 1 egg

UK: 200g all-purpose flour, ½ teaspoon baking soda, ½ teaspoon salt, 120g unsalted butter (softened), 100g granulated sugar, 100g brown sugar, 1 teaspoon vanilla extract, 125g smooth peanut butter, 1 egg

Instructions:

1. In the Ninja Foodi Cold & Hot Blender, combine softened butter, granulated sugar, brown sugar, vanilla extract, peanut butter, and egg.
2. Blend on the "Mix" function until creamy and well combined.
3. Add flour, baking soda, and salt to the blender.
4. Blend on the "Mix" function until a dough forms.
5. Transfer the cookie dough to a mixing bowl and fold in any additional mix-ins, such as chocolate chips or chopped nuts, if desired.
6. Preheat your oven to 350°F (180°C) and line a baking sheet with parchment paper.
7. Use a cookie scoop or spoon to portion out the dough onto the prepared baking sheet.
8. Flatten each cookie slightly with a fork.
9. Bake for 8-10 minutes or until the edges are lightly golden.
10. Allow the cookies to cool on the baking sheet for a few minutes before transferring them to a wire rack to cool completely.

Nutritional Info: (Per cookie) Calories: 150 | Fat: 8g | Carbs: 18g | Protein: 3g

Wholemeal Bread Dough

Prep: 15 mins | Cook: 25 mins | Serves: 1 loaf
ingredients:

US: 300g wholemeal flour, 200g all-purpose flour, 2 tablespoons honey, 2 tablespoons olive oil, 1 teaspoon salt, 1 teaspoon instant yeast, 300ml warm water

UK: 300g wholemeal flour, 200g all-purpose flour, 2 tablespoons honey, 2 tablespoons olive oil, 1 teaspoon salt, 1 teaspoon instant yeast, 300ml warm water

Instructions:

1. In the Ninja Foodi Cold & Hot Blender, combine wholemeal flour, all-purpose flour, honey, olive oil, salt, and instant yeast.
2. Blend on the "Dough" function until a dough forms.
3. Slowly add warm water while blending until the dough comes together and pulls away from the sides.
4. Transfer the dough to a lightly floured surface and knead for a few minutes until smooth.
5. Shape the dough into a loaf and place it in a greased loaf pan.
6. Cover the loaf pan with a clean kitchen towel and let the dough rise in a warm place for about 1 hour or until doubled in size.
7. Preheat your oven to 375°F (190°C).
8. Bake the bread for 25-30 minutes or until golden brown and sounds hollow when tapped on the bottom.
9. Remove the bread from the oven and let it cool in the pan for 10 minutes before transferring it to a wire rack to cool completely.
10. Slice and enjoy your homemade wholemeal bread!

Nutritional Info: (Per slice, based on 12 slices) Calories: 150 | Fat: 4g | Carbs: 25g | Protein: 5g

Lemon Blueberry Muffin Batter

Prep: 10 mins | Cook: 20 mins | Serves: 12 muffins

Ingredients:

US: 250g all-purpose flour, 150g sugar, 2 teaspoons baking powder, ½ teaspoon baking soda, ½ teaspoon salt, 120ml vegetable oil, 120ml milk, 2 eggs, 1 teaspoon vanilla extract, zest of 1 lemon, 150g fresh blueberries

UK: 250g all-purpose flour, 150g sugar, 2 teaspoons baking powder, ½ teaspoon baking soda, ½ teaspoon salt, 120ml vegetable oil, 120ml milk, 2 eggs, 1 teaspoon vanilla extract, zest of 1 lemon, 150g fresh blueberries

Instructions:

1. Preheat your oven to 375°F (190°C) and line a muffin tin with paper liners.
2. In the Ninja Foodi Cold & Hot Blender, combine flour, sugar, baking powder, baking soda, and salt.
3. Blend on the "Mix" function until well combined.
4. Add vegetable oil, milk, eggs, vanilla extract, and lemon zest to the blender.
5. Blend on the "Mix" function until smooth.
6. Gently fold in the fresh blueberries using a spatula.
7. Spoon the batter into the prepared muffin tin, filling each cup about ¾ full.
8. Bake for 18-20 minutes or until a toothpick inserted into the center comes out clean.
9. Remove the muffins from the oven and let them cool in the tin for 5 minutes before transferring them to a wire rack to cool completely.
10. Enjoy these lemony, blueberry delights!

Nutritional Info: (Per muffin) Calories: 200 | Fat: 8g | Carbs: 30g | Protein: 3g

Fudgy Brownie Batter

Prep: 10 mins | Cook: 25 mins | Serves: 16 brownies

Ingredients:

US: 200g unsalted butter, 200g granulated sugar, 3 eggs, 1 teaspoon vanilla extract, 80g all-purpose flour, 60g cocoa powder, ½ teaspoon salt, 100g chocolate chips

UK: 200g unsalted butter, 200g granulated sugar, 3 eggs, 1 teaspoon vanilla extract, 80g all-purpose flour, 60g cocoa powder, ½ teaspoon salt, 100g chocolate chips

Instructions:

1. Preheat your oven to 350°F (180°C) and line a baking pan with parchment paper.
2. In the Ninja Foodi Cold & Hot Blender, melt the butter.
3. Add granulated sugar, eggs, and vanilla extract to the blender.
4. Blend on the "Mix" function until well combined.
5. Add flour, cocoa powder, and salt to the blender.
6. Blend on the "Mix" function until smooth.
7. Fold in chocolate chips using a spatula.
8. Pour the batter into the prepared baking pan and spread it evenly.
9. Bake for 20-25 minutes or until a toothpick inserted into the centre comes out with a few moist crumbs.
10. Allow the brownies to cool in the pan before slicing them into squares.

Nutritional Info: (Per brownie) Calories: 200 | Fat: 10g | Carbs: 25g | Protein: 3g

Strawberry "Nice" Cream

Prep: 5 mins | Cook: 0 mins | Serves: 2
Ingredients:

US: 200g frozen strawberries, 2 ripe bananas, 60ml milk (optional)

UK: 200g frozen strawberries, 2 ripe bananas, 60ml milk (optional)

Instructions:
1. In the Ninja Foodi Cold & Hot Blender, combine frozen strawberries and ripe bananas.
2. Add milk if desired for a creamier consistency.
3. Blend on the "Ice Cream" function until smooth and creamy.
4. Serve immediately as soft-serve or transfer to a container and freeze for a firmer texture.
5. Enjoy this guilt-free treat!

Nutritional Info: (Per serving) Calories: 150 | Fat: 1g | Carbs: 35g | Protein: 2g

Homemade Almond Butter

Prep: 15 mins | Cook: 10 mins | Serves: 1 jar
Ingredients:

US: 300g almonds, ½ teaspoon salt, 1 tablespoon honey (optional)

UK: 300g almonds, ½ teaspoon salt, 1 tablespoon honey (optional)

Instructions:
1. Preheat your oven to 350°F (180°C) and spread almonds evenly on a baking sheet.
2. Roast almonds for 10 minutes, stirring halfway through, until fragrant and lightly golden.
3. Allow the almonds to cool slightly before transferring them to the Ninja Foodi Cold & Hot Blender.
4. Add salt and honey, if using, to the blender.
5. Blend on the "Nut Butter" function, scraping down the sides as needed, until smooth and creamy.
6. Transfer the almond butter to a sterilized jar or container.
7. Store at room temperature for up to two weeks or in the refrigerator for longer shelf life.
8. Enjoy your homemade almond butter on toast, in smoothies, or as a dip!

Nutritional Info: (Per tablespoon) Calories: 100 | Fat: 9g | Carbs: 3g | Protein: 4g

Cashew Milk for Baking

Prep: 5 mins | Cook: 0 mins | Serves: 2 cups

ingredients:

US: 100g raw cashews, 480ml water

UK: 100g raw cashews, 480ml water

Instructions:

1. Soak cashews in water for at least 4 hours or overnight.
2. Drain and rinse soaked cashews, then add them to the Ninja Foodi Cold & Hot Blender.
3. Add fresh water to the blender.
4. Blend on the "Milk" function until smooth and creamy.
5. Use cashew milk as a dairy-free alternative in baking recipes or smoothies.
6. Store leftover cashew milk in a sealed container in the refrigerator for up to 5 days.

Nutritional Info: (Per cup) Calories: 50 | Fat: 4g | Carbs: 2g | Protein: 2g

Savoury Lentil & Walnut Veggie Patties

Prep: 15 mins | Cook: 20 mins | Serves: 4
Ingredients:

US: 200g cooked lentils, 100g walnuts, 1 small onion, 2 garlic cloves, 1 tsp cumin, 1 tsp paprika, 1 tbsp soy sauce, salt, pepper, olive oil (for frying)

UK: 200g cooked lentils, 100g walnuts, 1 small onion, 2 garlic cloves, 1 tsp cumin, 1 tsp paprika, 1 tbsp soy sauce, salt, pepper, olive oil (for frying)

Instructions:

1. In your Ninja Foodi Cold & Hot Blender, combine cooked lentils, walnuts, chopped onion, minced garlic, cumin, paprika, soy sauce, salt, and pepper.
2. Blend on the "Chop" function until the mixture is well combined but still slightly chunky.
3. Shape the mixture into patties using your hands.
4. Heat olive oil in a skillet over medium heat.
5. Cook the lentil and walnut patties for about 4-5 minutes on each side until golden brown and crispy.
6. Serve the veggie patties on buns with your favourite toppings and condiments.

Nutritional Info: (Per serving) Calories: 250 | Fat: 15g | Carbs: 20g | Protein: 10g

Creamy Roasted Red Pepper Cashew Sauce

Prep: 10 mins | Cook: 20 mins | Serves: 4
Ingredients:

US: 2 large red bell peppers, 100g cashews (soaked), 2 garlic cloves, 1 tbsp lemon juice, 2 tbsp nutritional yeast, salt, pepper, olive oil

UK: 2 large red bell peppers, 100g cashews (soaked), 2 garlic cloves, 1 tbsp lemon juice, 2 tbsp nutritional yeast, salt, pepper, olive oil

Instructions:

1. Preheat your oven to 400°F (200°C) and line a baking sheet with parchment paper.
2. Place whole red bell peppers on the baking sheet and roast for 20-25 minutes until charred and softened.
3. Remove the peppers from the oven and let them cool slightly before peeling off the skins and removing the seeds.

4. In the Ninja Foodi Cold & Hot Blender, combine roasted red peppers, soaked cashews, minced garlic, lemon juice, nutritional yeast, salt, and pepper.
5. Blend on the "Puree" function until smooth and creamy.
6. Heat a little olive oil in a saucepan and pour in the red pepper cashew sauce.
7. Cook for a few minutes until heated through.
8. Serve the sauce over pasta, grilled vegetables, or as a dip for crusty bread.

Nutritional Info: (Per serving) Calories: 180 | Fat: 12g | Carbs: 15g | Protein: 6g

Flavorful Portobello Mushroom "Meatballs"

Prep: 15 mins | Cook: 25 mins | Serves: 4
Ingredients:

US: 500g portobello mushrooms, 1 onion, 2 garlic cloves, 50g breadcrumbs, 1 tsp dried oregano, 1 tsp dried basil, salt, pepper, olive oil

UK: 500g portobello mushrooms, 1 onion, 2 garlic cloves, 50g breadcrumbs, 1 tsp dried oregano, 1 tsp dried basil, salt, pepper, olive oil

Instructions:
1. Preheat your oven to 375°F (190°C) and line a baking sheet with parchment paper.
2. Clean the portobello mushrooms and remove the stems.
3. Finely chop mushrooms, onion, and garlic.
4. In a frying pan, heat olive oil over medium heat, add chopped onion and garlic, sauté until translucent.
5. Add chopped mushrooms, dried oregano, dried basil, salt, and pepper, cook until mushrooms release moisture and become tender.
6. Remove from heat, let it cool slightly, then transfer to the Ninja Foodi Cold & Hot Blender.
7. Add breadcrumbs and pulse until well combined.
8. Shape the mixture into meatballs using your hands.
9. Place meatballs on the prepared baking sheet and bake for 20-25 minutes until golden brown.
10. Serve hot with your favorite sauce or pasta.

Nutritional Info: (Per serving) Calories: 150 | Fat: 5g | Carbs: 20g | Protein: 7g

Authentic Thai Red Curry Paste

Prep: 15 mins | Cook: 0 mins | Makes: Approx. 1 cup
Ingredients:

US: 6 dried red chillies, 2 shallots, 4 garlic cloves, 2 lemongrass stalks, 1-inch piece of galangal (or ginger), 1 tbsp coriander seeds, 1 tsp cumin seeds, 1 tsp paprika, 1 tbsp tomato puree, 1 tbsp soy sauce, 1 tbsp lime juice, salt

UK: 6 dried red chillies, 2 shallots, 4 garlic cloves, 2 lemongrass stalks, 1-inch piece of galangal (or ginger), 1 tbsp coriander seeds, 1 tsp cumin seeds, 1 tsp paprika, 1 tbsp tomato puree, 1 tbsp soy sauce, 1 tbsp lime juice, salt

Instructions:

1. Soak dried red chillies in hot water for 15 minutes to rehydrate.
2. Meanwhile, peel and roughly chop shallots, garlic, lemongrass, and galangal.
3. In the Ninja Foodi Cold & Hot Blender, combine soaked red chillies, chopped shallots, garlic, lemongrass, galangal, coriander seeds, cumin seeds, paprika, tomato puree, soy sauce, lime juice, and a pinch of salt.
4. Blend on the "Puree" function until smooth, scraping down the sides as needed.
5. Transfer the Thai red curry paste to a clean jar and store it in the refrigerator for up to two weeks.

Nutritional Info: (Per serving) Calories: 25 | Fat: 0.5g | Carbs: 5g | Protein: 1g

Homemade Falafel Mix

Prep: 15 mins | Cook: 10 mins | Makes: 12 falafel
Ingredients:

US: 1 can (400g) chickpeas, 1 small onion, 2 garlic cloves, 1 tbsp chopped fresh parsley, 1 tbsp chopped fresh coriander, 1 tsp ground cumin, 1 tsp ground coriander, 1/4 tsp cayenne pepper, 1 tbsp all-purpose flour, salt, pepper, vegetable oil (for frying)

UK: 1 can (400g) chickpeas, 1 small onion, 2 garlic cloves, 1 tbsp chopped fresh parsley, 1 tbsp chopped fresh coriander, 1 tsp ground cumin, 1 tsp ground coriander, 1/4 tsp cayenne pepper, 1 tbsp all-purpose flour, salt, pepper, vegetable oil (for frying)

Instructions:

1. Rinse and drain chickpeas, then pat them dry with paper towels.
2. In the Ninja Foodi Cold & Hot Blender, combine chickpeas, chopped onion, garlic cloves, parsley, coriander, ground cumin, ground coriander, cayenne pepper, flour, salt, and pepper.

3. Pulse until the mixture comes together but is still slightly coarse.
4. Transfer the mixture to a bowl and refrigerate for 30 minutes to firm up.
5. Shape the falafel mixture into small balls or patties.
6. Heat vegetable oil in a frying pan over medium heat.
7. Fry the falafel in batches for 3-4 minutes on each side until golden brown and crispy.
8. Remove from the pan and drain on paper towels.
9. Serve the falafel hot with hummus, tahini sauce, or in pita bread with salad.

Nutritional Info: (Per serving - 3 falafel) Calories: 200 | Fat: 8g | Carbs: 25g | Protein: 7g

Creamy Spinach Artichoke Pesto

Prep: 10 mins | Cook: 0 mins | Makes: Approx. 1 cup
Ingredients:

US: 2 cups fresh spinach leaves, 1 cup canned artichoke hearts, 1/4 cup grated Parmesan cheese, 1/4 cup pine nuts, 2 garlic cloves, 1 tbsp lemon juice, 1/4 cup olive oil, salt, pepper

UK: 2 cups fresh spinach leaves, 1 cup canned artichoke hearts, 1/4 cup grated Parmesan cheese, 1/4 cup pine nuts, 2 garlic cloves, 1 tbsp lemon juice, 1/4 cup olive oil, salt, pepper

Instructions:
1. Drain and roughly chop canned artichoke hearts.
2. In the Ninja Foodi Cold & Hot Blender, combine spinach leaves, chopped artichoke hearts, grated Parmesan cheese, pine nuts, minced garlic cloves, lemon juice, olive oil, salt, and pepper.
3. Blend on the "Puree" function until smooth and creamy, scraping down the sides as needed.
4. If the pesto is too thick, add more olive oil until desired consistency is reached.
5. Taste and adjust seasoning if necessary.
6. Transfer the spinach artichoke pesto to a clean jar and refrigerate for up to one week.

Nutritional Info: (Per serving) Calories: 120 | Fat: 10g | Carbs: 5g | Protein: 3g

Authentic Massaman Curry Sauce

Prep: 10 mins | Cook: 10 mins | Makes: Approx. 2 cups
Ingredients:

US: 2 shallots, 4 garlic cloves, 1-inch piece of ginger, 2 red chillies, 2 lemongrass stalks, 1 tbsp coriander seeds, 1 tsp cumin seeds, 1/2 tsp ground cinnamon, 1/4 tsp ground cloves, 1/4 tsp ground nutmeg, 1/4 tsp ground cardamom, 1/4 cup roasted peanuts, 1 tbsp tomato puree, 1 tbsp tamarind paste, 1 can (400ml) coconut milk, 1 tbsp brown sugar, 1 tbsp fish sauce (or soy sauce for vegetarian), salt

UK: 2 shallots, 4 garlic cloves, 1-inch piece of ginger, 2 red chillies, 2 lemongrass stalks, 1 tbsp coriander seeds, 1 tsp cumin seeds, 1/2 tsp ground cinnamon, 1/4 tsp ground cloves, 1/4 tsp ground nutmeg, 1/4 tsp ground cardamom, 1/4 cup roasted peanuts, 1 tbsp tomato puree, 1 tbsp tamarind paste, 1 can (400ml) coconut milk, 1 tbsp brown sugar, 1 tbsp fish sauce (or soy sauce for vegetarian), salt

Instructions:

1. Peel and roughly chop shallots, garlic cloves, ginger, and red chillies.
2. In the Ninja Foodi Cold & Hot Blender, combine chopped shallots, garlic cloves, ginger, red chillies, lemongrass, coriander seeds, cumin seeds, ground cinnamon, ground cloves, ground nutmeg, ground cardamom, roasted peanuts, tomato puree, tamarind paste, coconut milk, brown sugar, fish sauce, and a pinch of salt.
3. Blend on the "Puree" function until smooth.
4. Transfer the mixture to a saucepan and bring to a gentle simmer over medium heat.
5. Cook for 8-10 minutes, stirring occasionally, until the sauce thickens slightly.
6. Taste and adjust seasoning if needed.
7. Remove from heat and use the Massaman curry sauce as a base for your favourite curry dishes.

Nutritional Info: (Per serving - 1/4 cup) Calories: 150 | Fat: 12g | Carbs: 8g | Protein: 3g

Beer Batter for Frying

Prep: 5 mins | Cook: 0 mins | Makes: Approx. 1 cup
ingredients:

US: 1 cup all-purpose flour, 1 tsp baking powder, 1/2 tsp salt, 1/2 cup beer (lager or ale), 1 egg

UK: 1 cup all-purpose flour, 1 tsp baking powder, 1/2 tsp salt, 1/2 cup beer (lager or ale), 1 egg

Instructions:

1. In a mixing bowl, whisk together all-purpose flour, baking powder, and salt.
2. Make a well in the center of the dry ingredients and add the beer and egg.
3. Whisk until smooth and well combined.
4. Let the beer batter rest for 10-15 minutes before using.
5. Dip your desired food items (such as fish, shrimp, or vegetables) into the beer batter, ensuring they are evenly coated.
6. Fry in hot oil (around 180°C/350°F) until golden brown and crispy.
7. Remove from the oil and drain on paper towels before serving.

Nutritional Info: (Per serving - 1/4 cup) Calories: 110 | Fat: 1g | Carbs: 20g | Protein: 4g

Sun-Dried Tomato Pesto

Prep: 10 mins | Cook: 0 mins | Makes: Approx. 1 cupIngredients:

US: 1 cup sun-dried tomatoes (packed in oil), 2 garlic cloves, 1/4 cup grated Parmesan cheese, 1/4 cup pine nuts, 1/4 cup fresh basil leaves, 1/4 cup olive oil, salt, pepper

UK: 1 cup sun-dried tomatoes (packed in oil), 2 garlic cloves, 1/4 cup grated Parmesan cheese, 1/4 cup pine nuts, 1/4 cup fresh basil leaves, 1/4 cup olive oil, salt, pepper

Instructions:

1. Drain the sun-dried tomatoes from the oil and pat them dry with paper towels.
2. In the Ninja Foodi Cold & Hot Blender, combine sun-dried tomatoes, peeled garlic cloves, grated Parmesan cheese, pine nuts, fresh basil leaves, olive oil, salt, and pepper.
3. Blend on the "Puree" function until smooth, scraping down the sides as needed.
4. Taste and adjust seasoning if necessary.
5. Transfer the sun-dried tomato pesto to a clean jar and refrigerate for up to one week.

Nutritional Info: (Per serving) Calories: 120 | Fat: 10g | Carbs: 5g | Protein: 3g

Greek Lentil Fritters

Prep: 15 mins | Cook: 15 mins | Makes: 12 fritters
Ingredients:

US: 1 cup cooked lentils, 1 small onion, 2 garlic cloves, 1/4 cup chopped fresh parsley, 1/4 cup crumbled feta cheese, 1 tsp dried oregano, 1/2 tsp ground cumin, 1/4 cup breadcrumbs, 1 egg, salt, pepper, olive oil (for frying)

UK: 1 cup cooked lentils, 1 small onion, 2 garlic cloves, 1/4 cup chopped fresh parsley, 1/4 cup crumbled feta cheese, 1 tsp dried oregano, 1/2 tsp ground cumin, 1/4 cup breadcrumbs, 1 egg, salt, pepper, olive oil (for frying)

Instructions:

1. In the Ninja Foodi Cold & Hot Blender, combine cooked lentils, chopped onion, minced garlic cloves, chopped parsley, crumbled feta cheese, dried oregano, ground cumin, breadcrumbs, and egg.
2. Pulse until the mixture comes together but is still slightly chunky.
3. Transfer the lentil mixture to a bowl and season with salt and pepper to taste.
4. Heat olive oil in a frying pan over medium heat.
5. Scoop spoonfuls of the lentil mixture and shape them into fritters.

6. Fry the fritters in batches for 3-4 minutes on each side until golden brown and crispy.
7. Remove from the pan and drain on paper towels.

Serve the Greek lentil fritters hot with tzatziki sauce or a squeeze of lemon.

Nutritional Info: (Per serving - 2 fritters) Calories: 150 | Fat: 8g | Carbs: 15g | Protein: 7g

Mixed Berry Antioxidant Blast

Prep: 5 mins | Blend: 1 min | Serves: 2
Ingredients:

US: 1 cup mixed berries (strawberries, blueberries, and raspberries), 1 ripe banana, 1/2 cup spinach, leaves, 1/2 cup coconut water, 1 tablespoon chia seeds, 1 tablespoon honey (optional)

UK: 150g mixed berries (strawberries, blueberries, raspberries), 1 ripe banana, 40g spinach leaves, 120ml coconut water, 15g chia seeds, 15ml honey (optional)

Instructions:

1. Add mixed berries, banana, spinach leaves, coconut water, chia seeds, and honey (if using) into the blender pitcher of your Ninja Foodi Cold & Hot Blender.
2. Secure the lid and select the "Smoothie" function.
3. Blend until smooth, about 1 minute.
4. Pour into glasses and serve immediately.

Nutritional Info: (per serving) Calories: 120 | Fat: 2g | Carbs: 25g | Protein: 3g

Vanilla Protein Boost

Prep: 5 mins | Blend: 1 min | Serves: 1
Ingredients:

US & UK: 1 scoop vanilla protein powder, 1 ripe banana, 1 tablespoon almond butter, 1 cup almond milk, 1/2 teaspoon vanilla extract, Ice cubes (optional).

Instructions:

1. Place vanilla protein powder, banana, almond butter, almond milk, and vanilla extract into the blender pitcher of your Ninja Foodi Cold & Hot Blender.
2. Secure the lid and select the "Smoothie" function.
3. Blend until smooth, about 1 minute.
4. Add ice cubes if desired and blend again until creamy.
5. Pour into a glass and enjoy your protein-packed smoothie.

Nutritional Info: (per serving) Calories: 350 | Fat: 14g | Carbs: 30g | Protein: 25g

Green Detox Zinger

Prep: 5 mins | Blend: 1 min | Serves: 2
Ingredients:
US & UK: 2 cups spinach leaves, 1 cucumber, chopped, 1 green apple, cored and chopped, 1/2 lemon, peeled, 1 tablespoon fresh ginger, grated, 1 cup coconut water, Ice cubes (optional)

Instructions:
1. Add spinach leaves, cucumber, green apple, lemon, ginger, and coconut water into the blender pitcher of your Ninja Foodi Cold & Hot Blender.
2. Secure the lid and select the "Smoothie" function.
3. Blend until smooth, about 1 minute.
4. Add ice cubes if desired and blend again until well combined.
5. Pour into glasses and serve immediately for a refreshing detox drink.

Nutritional Info: (per serving) Calories: 90 | Fat: 0g | Carbs: 22g | Protein: 3g

Turmeric Ginger Wellness Shot

Prep: 5 mins | Blend: 1 min | Serves: 2
Ingredients:
US & UK: 2 tablespoons fresh turmeric, grated, 1 tablespoon fresh ginger, grated, Juice of 1 lemon Pinch of black pepper, Pinch of cayenne pepper (optional), 1 cup water.

Instructions:
1. Place fresh turmeric, ginger, lemon juice, black pepper, cayenne pepper (if using), and water into the blender pitcher of your Ninja Foodi Cold & Hot Blender.
2. Secure the lid and select the "Extract" function.
3. Blend until smooth, about 1 minute.
4. Strain the mixture through a fine mesh sieve to remove any fibrous bits.
5. Pour the wellness shot into shot glasses and consume immediately.

Nutritional Info: (per serving) Calories: 15 | Fat: 0g | Carbs: 4g | Protein: 0g

Chocolate Maca Energizer

Prep: 5 mins | Blend: 1 min | Serves: 1

Ingredients:

US & UK: 1 cup almond milk, 1 tablespoon cocoa powder, 1 tablespoon maca powder, 1 tablespoon maple syrup or honey, 1/2 teaspoon vanilla extract, Ice cubes (optional).

Instructions:

1. Add almond milk, cocoa powder, maca powder, maple syrup or honey, and vanilla extract into the blender pitcher of your Ninja Foodi Cold & Hot Blender.
2. Secure the lid and select the "Smoothie" function.
3. Blend until smooth, about 1 minute.
4. Add ice cubes if desired and blend again until creamy.
5. Pour into a glass and enjoy your chocolatey energy boost.

Nutritional Info: (per serving) Calories: 150 | Fat: 5g | Carbs: 25g | Protein: 3g

Espresso Almond Energizer

Prep: 5 mins | Blend: 1 min | Serves: 1

Ingredients:

US & UK: 1 shot espresso, cooled, 1 cup almond milk, 1 tablespoon almond butter, 1 tablespoon maple syrup or honey, Ice cubes (optional).

Instructions:

1. Brew espresso and let it cool to room temperature.
2. Add cooled espresso, almond milk, almond butter, and maple syrup or honey into the blender pitcher of your Ninja Foodi Cold & Hot Blender.
3. Secure the lid and select the "Smoothie" function.
4. Blend until smooth, about 1 minute.
5. Add ice cubes if desired and blend again until creamy.
6. Pour into a glass and enjoy your espresso-infused energy drink.

Nutritional Info: (per serving) Calories: 150 | Fat: 5g | Carbs: 20g | Protein: 3g

Coconut Collagen Creamer

Prep: 5 mins | Blend: 1 min | Serves: 4

Ingredients:

US & UK: 1 can (400ml) coconut milk, 2 tablespoons collagen peptides, 1 tablespoon maple syrup or honey, 1 teaspoon vanilla extract.

Instructions:

1. Add coconut milk, collagen peptides, maple syrup or honey, and vanilla extract into the blender pitcher of your Ninja Foodi Cold & Hot Blender.
2. Secure the lid and select the "Blend" function.
3. Blend until smooth, about 1 minute.
4. Transfer the creamer to a jar or bottle with a tight-fitting lid.
5. Store in the refrigerator for up to 1 week.
6. Shake well before using and add to coffee or tea for a creamy, collagen-rich boost.

Nutritional Info: (per serving) Calories: 180 | Fat: 15g | Carbs: 5g | Protein: 5g

Golden Milk Protein Shake

Prep: 5 mins | Blend: 1 min | Serves: 1

Ingredients:

US & UK: 1 cup almond milk, 1 scoop vanilla protein powder, 1 teaspoon ground turmeric, 1/2 teaspoon ground cinnamon, Pinch of black pepper, 1 tablespoon maple syrup or honey.

Instructions:

1. Add almond milk, vanilla protein powder, ground turmeric, ground cinnamon, black pepper, and maple syrup or honey into the blender pitcher of your Ninja Foodi Cold & Hot Blender.
2. Secure the lid and select the "Smoothie" function.
3. Blend until smooth, about 1 minute.
4. Pour into a glass and enjoy your creamy and nutritious golden milk protein shake.

Nutritional Info: (per serving) Calories: 200 | Fat: 3g | Carbs: 20g | Protein: 25g

Beet & Cherry Recovery Tonic

Prep: 5 mins | Blend: 1 min | Serves: 2

Ingredients:

US: 1 small beet, peeled and chopped, 1 cup pitted cherries, 1 cup coconut water, Juice of 1/2 lemon.

UK: 150g small beet, peeled and chopped, 150g pitted cherries, 240ml coconut water, Juice of 1/2 lemon.

Instructions:

Add beet, cherries, coconut water, and lemon juice into the blender pitcher of your Ninja Foodi Cold & Hot Blender.

Secure the lid and select the "Smoothie" function.

Blend until smooth, about 1 minute.

Pour into glasses and serve immediately for a refreshing recovery tonic.

Nutritional Info: (per serving) Calories: 100 | Fat: 0g | Carbs: 25g | Protein: 2g

Probiotic Coconut Kefir Blend

Prep: 5 mins | Blend: 1 min | Serves: 2

Ingredients:

US & UK: 1 cup coconut water kefir, 1 cup mixed berries (strawberries, blueberries, raspberries), 1 tablespoon honey, 1/2 teaspoon vanilla extract, Ice cubes (optional).

Instructions:

1. Add coconut water kefir, mixed berries, honey, and vanilla extract into the blender pitcher of your Ninja Foodi Cold & Hot Blender.
2. Secure the lid and select the "Smoothie" function.
3. Blend until smooth, about 1 minute.
4. Add ice cubes if desired and blend again until well combined.
5. Pour into glasses and serve immediately for a probiotic-rich and refreshing beverage.

Nutritional Info: (per serving) Calories: 70 | Fat: 0g | Carbs: 18g | Protein: 1g

Chapter 10: Sips & Tonics

Strawberry Margaritas

Prep: 5 mins | Blend: 1 min | Serves: 2
Ingredients:
US: 2 cups strawberries, hulled, 1/4 cup fresh lime juice, 1/4 cup tequila, 2 tablespoons triple sec, 1 tablespoon agave nectar, Ice cubes.
UK: 320g strawberries, hulled, 60ml fresh lime juice, 60ml tequila, 30ml triple sec, 15ml agave nectar, Ice cubes,

Instructions:

1. Add strawberries, lime juice, tequila, triple sec, and agave nectar into the blender pitcher of your Ninja Foodi Cold & Hot Blender.
2. Secure the lid and select the "Frozen Drink" function.
3. Blend until smooth, about 1 minute.
4. Add ice cubes to adjust consistency and blend again if needed.
5. Rim glasses with salt or sugar if desired.
6. Pour margaritas into glasses and serve with a lime wedge.

Nutritional Info: (per serving) Calories: 150 | Fat: 0g | Carbs: 20g | Protein: 1g

Hot Vanilla Latte

Prep: 5 mins | Blend: 2 mins | Serves: 1
Ingredients:
US & UK: 1 cup milk (dairy or plant-based), 1 tablespoon vanilla extract, 1 tablespoon honey or sugar, 1 shot espresso or 1/2 cup strong brewed coffee.

Instructions:

1. Pour milk, vanilla extract, and honey or sugar into the blender pitcher of your Ninja Foodi Cold & Hot Blender.
2. Secure the lid and select the "Hot Drink" function.
3. Blend until heated through and frothy, about 2 minutes.
4. Meanwhile, brew espresso or coffee.
5. Pour the hot vanilla milk into a mug and add espresso or coffee.
6. Stir well and enjoy your comforting hot vanilla latte.

Nutritional Info: (per serving) Calories: 150 | Fat: 5g | Carbs: 20g | Protein: 8g

Passionfruit Mojito Mocktail

Prep: 5 mins | Blend: 1 min | Serves: 2
Ingredients:
US & UK: Pulp of 2 passionfruits, 1/4 cup fresh lime juice, 1/4 cup fresh mint leaves, 2 tablespoons honey or sugar, 1 cup sparkling water, Ice cubes

Instructions:

1. Scoop out the pulp of the passionfruits and add it to the blender pitcher of your Ninja Foodi Cold & Hot Blender.
2. Add lime juice, mint leaves, honey or sugar, and sparkling water.
3. Secure the lid and select the "Smoothie" function.
4. Blend until well combined, about 1 minute.
5. Fill glasses with ice cubes and pour the passionfruit mojito mocktail over the ice.
6. Garnish with extra mint leaves and enjoy your refreshing mocktail.

Nutritional Info: (per serving) Calories: 70 | Fat: 0g | Carbs: 20g | Protein: 1g

Matcha Green Tea Frappe

Prep: 5 mins | Blend: 2 mins | Serves: 1
Ingredients:
US & UK: 1 cup milk (dairy or plant-based), 2 teaspoons matcha green tea powder, 1 tablespoon honey or sugar, 1/2 teaspoon vanilla extract, Ice cubes, Whipped cream (optional).

Instructions:

1. Pour milk, matcha green tea powder, honey or sugar, and vanilla extract into the blender pitcher of your Ninja Foodi Cold & Hot Blender.
2. Secure the lid and select the "Frozen Drink" function.
3. Blend until smooth and creamy, about 2 minutes.
4. Add ice cubes to achieve desired consistency and blend again if needed.
5. Pour the matcha frappe into a glass.
6. Top with whipped cream if desired and enjoy your indulgent matcha treat.

Nutritional Info: (per serving) Calories: 150 | Fat: 5g | Carbs: 20g | Protein: 8g

Buttered Rum

Prep: 5 mins | Blend: 2 mins | Serves: 1
Ingredients:
US & UK: 1 cup hot water, 2 tablespoons unsalted butter, 2 tablespoons brown sugar, 1/4 teaspoon ground cinnamon, 1/4 teaspoon ground nutmeg, 1 shot dark rum, Whipped cream (optional)

Instructions:
1. Heat water until hot but not boiling.
2. Add hot water, unsalted butter, brown sugar, ground cinnamon, and ground nutmeg into the blender pitcher of your Ninja Foodi Cold & Hot Blender.
3. Secure the lid and select the "Hot Drink" function.
4. Blend until well combined and frothy, about 2 minutes.
5. Pour the buttered rum mixture into a mug and add a shot of dark rum.
6. Stir gently to combine.
7. Top with whipped cream if desired and enjoy your cozy buttered rum.

Nutritional Info: (per serving) Calories: 200 | Fat: 10g | Carbs: 20g | Protein: 0g

Ginger Lemongrass Refresher

Prep: 5 mins | Blend: 2 mins | Serves: 2
Ingredients:
US & UK: 2 stalks lemongrass, trimmed and chopped, 1 tablespoon fresh ginger, grated, 1/4 cup fresh lime juice, 2 tablespoons honey or sugar, 2 cups cold water, Ice cubes, Fresh mint leaves for garnish.

Instructions:
1. Place lemongrass, fresh ginger, lime juice, honey or sugar, and cold water into the blender pitcher of your Ninja Foodi Cold & Hot Blender.
2. Secure the lid and select the "Smoothie" function.
3. Blend until the ingredients are well combined and the lemongrass and ginger are finely blended, about 2 minutes.
4. Strain the mixture through a fine mesh sieve to remove any fibrous bits.
5. Fill glasses with ice cubes and pour the ginger lemongrass refresher over the ice.
6. Garnish with fresh mint leaves and serve immediately.

Nutritional Info: (per serving) Calories: 60 | Fat: 0g | Carbs: 15g | Protein: 0g

Lavender Lemonade

Prep: 10 mins | Blend: 2 mins | Serves: 4
Ingredients:
US & UK: 4 cups water, 1/4 cup dried culinary lavender, 1 cup fresh lemon juice, 1/2 cup honey or sugar, Ice cubes, Lemon slices for garnish.

Instructions:

1. In a saucepan, bring water to a boil.
2. Remove from heat and add dried culinary lavender.
3. Let steep for 5-7 minutes, then strain the lavender-infused water into a bowl and let it cool to room temperature.
4. In the blender pitcher of your Ninja Foodi Cold & Hot Blender, combine the lavender-infused water, fresh lemon juice, and honey or sugar.
5. Secure the lid and select the "Smoothie" function.
6. Blend until the mixture is smooth and well combined, about 2 minutes.
7. Fill glasses with ice cubes and pour the lavender lemonade over the ice.
8. Garnish with lemon slices and serve chilled.

Nutritional Info: (per serving) Calories: 80 | Fat: 0g | Carbs: 20g | Protein: 0g

Salted Caramel White Russian

Prep: 5 mins | Blend: 2 mins | Serves: 1
Ingredients:
US & UK: 1 shot vodka, 1 shot coffee liqueur, 1/4 cup milk (dairy or plant-based), 2 tablespoons caramel sauce, Pinch of sea salt, Ice cubes, Whipped cream for garnish (optional).

Instructions:

1. In a glass, combine vodka, coffee liqueur, milk, caramel sauce, and a pinch of sea salt.
2. Stir until well combined.
3. Pour the mixture into the blender pitcher of your Ninja Foodi Cold & Hot Blender.
4. Secure the lid and select the "Frozen Drink" function.
5. Blend until smooth and creamy, about 2 minutes.
6. Fill a glass with ice cubes and pour the salted caramel white Russian over the ice.
7. Garnish with whipped cream if desired and enjoy your indulgent cocktail.

Nutritional Info: (per serving) Calories: 250 | Fat: 3g | Carbs: 30g | Protein: 1g

Turmeric Tonic

Prep: 5 mins | Blend: 1 min | Serves: 2
Ingredients:
US: 2 cups coconut water, 1 tablespoon fresh turmeric, grated, 1 tablespoon fresh ginger, grated, Juice of 1 lemon, Pinch of black pepper.
UK: 480ml coconut water, 15g fresh turmeric, grated, 15g fresh ginger, grated, Juice of 1 lemon, Pinch of black pepper.

Instructions:
1. Add coconut water, fresh turmeric, fresh ginger, lemon juice, and black pepper into the blender pitcher of your Ninja Foodi Cold & Hot Blender.
2. Secure the lid and select the "Smoothie" function.
3. Blend until smooth, about 1 minute.
4. Pour the turmeric tonic into glasses and serve chilled or over ice.

Nutritional Info: (per serving) Calories: 60 | Fat: 0g | Carbs: 15g | Protein: 1g

Blackberry Rosemary Spritzer

Prep: 10 mins | Blend: 2 mins | Serves: 4
Ingredients:
US & UK: 2 cups blackberries, 2 sprigs fresh rosemary, 1/4 cup honey or sugar
2 tablespoons fresh lemon juice, 4 cups sparkling water, Ice cubes, Blackberries and rosemary sprigs for garnish.

Instructions:
1. In a saucepan, combine blackberries, fresh rosemary, honey or sugar, and fresh lemon juice.
2. Heat over medium heat, stirring occasionally, until the blackberries break down and the mixture is syrupy, about 5-7 minutes.
3. Remove from heat and let it cool slightly.
4. Strain the blackberry mixture through a fine mesh sieve into a bowl, pressing down on the solids to extract all the liquid.
5. In the blender pitcher of your Ninja Foodi Cold & Hot Blender, combine the blackberry syrup and sparkling water.
6. Secure the lid and select the "Smoothie" function.
7. Blend until well combined, about 2 minutes.
8. Fill glasses with ice cubes and pour the blackberry rosemary spritzer over the ice.
9. Garnish with blackberries and rosemary sprigs and serve immediately.

Nutritional Info: (per serving) Calories: 60 | Fat: 0g | Carbs: 15g | Protein: 0g

Calculating Calories, Macros, etc.

As someone passionate about healthy eating and nutrition, I know how important it is to understand the nutritional value of the foods we consume. With the Ninja Foodi Cold & Hot Blender, you have the power to create incredibly nutritious and delicious blends right at home. However, it's also essential to be mindful of portion sizes and macronutrient ratios to ensure you're fueling your body in a balanced way.

One of the greatest advantages of blending your meals and snacks is that you have complete control over the ingredients and can easily calculate the nutritional information. Whether you're tracking macros for fitness goals, managing a specific dietary condition, or simply want to make informed choices, here's how to break down the nutrition in your blended creations.

Calorie Counting

To determine the total calories in your blend, you'll need to know the calorie content of each ingredient. Many food packaging lists calories per serving, or you can easily look up calorie counts online or in nutrition databases. Simply add up the calories from all the ingredients based on the amounts used, and you'll have the total calorie count for your blend.

For example, let's say you're making a smoothie with:

- 1 banana (105 calories)
- 1 cup spinach (7 calories)
- 1 cup almond milk (30 calories)
- 1 tablespoon peanut butter (95 calories)

The total calorie count for this smoothie would be 105 + 7 + 30 + 95 = 237 calories.

Calculating Macros

In addition to calories, many people also like to track their macronutrient intake – that is, the grams of protein, carbohydrates, and fats in their diet. Again, you can find this information on food labels or online databases and simply add up the macros from each ingredient.

Continuing with our smoothie example:

- Banana: 27g carbs, 1g protein, 0g fat
- Spinach: 1g carb, 1g protein, 0g fat
- Almond milk: 1g carb, 1g protein, 2.5g fat
- Peanut butter: 3g carb, 8g protein, 16g fat

The total macros for this smoothie would be:

32g carbs, 11g protein, 18.5g fat

This information can be invaluable for those following specific dietary protocols or simply trying to achieve their macro targets.

Of course, tracking every single nutrient can quickly become tedious. Thankfully, there are many great apps and online calculators that can do the math for you once you input the ingredients and amounts. I highly recommend using a tool like this, especially when you're first getting started with nutritional tracking.

Catering to Dietary Needs

One of the best things about blending your own creations at home is the ability to cater to any dietary needs or preferences you may have. Whether you're vegan, gluten-free, nut-free, or managing a condition like diabetes, the Ninja Foodi gives you full control over what goes into your blends.

For example, those following a plant-based diet can easily make delicious dairy-free milk, smoothies, and creamy soups using nut/seed milk, coconut milk or yoghurt, avocado, and other vegan ingredients.

If you need to avoid gluten, simply skip any gluten-containing grains and flour when baking or making bread in the blender. Oats, nut flour, and seeds can be great gluten-free alternatives.

For those monitoring sugar intake, you can use low-glycemic fruits like berries, or opt for sugar substitutes like monk fruit or stevia. Veggies and greens can add nutrition without spiking blood sugar.

The possibilities are truly endless when it comes to catering the Ninja Blender recipes to your specific needs and preferences. I recommend keeping a list of your dietary must-haves or must-avoids, and referring to it when planning out recipes and ingredients.

Blender-Friendly Ingredient Swaps

In addition to accounting for dietary restrictions, some general ingredient swaps can help make your blends more blender-friendly in terms of taste, texture, and nutrition. Here are some of my top substitution tips:

Thickeners

If a smoothie or sauce blend is too thin, you can thicken it up by adding:
- Ripe avocado or avocado puree
- Nut or seed butter
- Oats or oat flour
- Chia seeds or flaxseeds
- Soft tofu
- Yogurt or kefir

Healthy Fats

For rich, creamy textures from healthy fats try:
- Coconut milk or cream
- Nut or seed milk/butter
- Olives or olive oil
- Avocado
- Ground flax or chia seeds

Protein Boosters

Need an extra protein punch? Blend in:
- Nut or seed butter
- Protein powder

- Greek yoghurt or cottage cheese
- Silken tofu
- Cooked chicken, turkey or lean beef
- Beans or lentils

Sweeteners

For natural sweetness without refined sugar, use:
- Bananas or dates
- Maple syrup or honey
- Unsweetened applesauce
- Vanilla extract
- Cinnamon or spices

The blender allows you to get creative with nutrient-dense whole-food ingredients such as thickeners, binders, and flavour enhancers. Don't be afraid to experiment with different combos to achieve your desired taste and texture.

Overall, paying attention to nutrition is essential for maintaining a healthy, balanced lifestyle. With a little knowledge of how to calculate macros and cater to your personal needs, the Ninja blender can be an incredible tool for crafting delicious, precisely optimised blends. Let's keep exploring the world of nutritious blending!

Conclusion

Wow, we've covered so much invaluable information about the Ninja Foodi Cold & Hot Blender in these preliminary pages! From getting to know the powerful features of this innovative kitchen appliance to mastering essential blending techniques, you now have a solid foundation to start whipping up incredibly delicious and nutritious blends like a pro.

But what sets the Ninja Foodi apart is its versatility in creating both hot and cold blends with ease. That dual functionality opens up a world of culinary possibilities, whether you're in the mood for a frosty smoothie, a piping hot soup, a decadent frozen treat, or a savoury blended sauce.

With the tips we discussed on calculating nutritional information and catering to specific dietary needs, you can feel confident that your blends are not only delicious but also perfectly tailored to your personal health goals and requirements.

I truly believe that the Ninja Foodi Cold & Hot Blender has the power to revolutionize the way you approach meal prep and healthy eating. With this incredible kitchen companion by your side, you'll be able to whip up nutritious, wholesome meals and snacks with ease, all while exploring new flavours and textures.

Of course, we've only just scratched the surface of what this amazing blender is capable of. In the chapters ahead, we'll dive deep into a world of mouthwatering recipes spanning everything from smoothies and juices to savoury mains, frozen treats, and beyond.

Get ready to be inspired, get creative, and blend! I can't wait to join you on this delicious and nutritious journey with the Ninja Foodi Cold & Hot Blender as your trusty culinary companion.

So grab your blender jug, gather your favourite fresh ingredients, and let's get started on crafting some truly special blends together. Here's to a world of new flavours, better health, and endless blending possibilities!

Printed in Great Britain
by Amazon

53445896R00044